LEARN FLASK

From Fundamentals to
Practical Applications

Diego Rodrigues

MASTERTECH
LEARN FLASK
From Fundamentals to Practical Applications

2025 Edition
Author: Diego Rodrigues

Published by StudioD21.

Important Note

The codes and scripts presented in this book aim to illustrate the concepts discussed in the chapters, serving as practical examples. These examples were developed in custom, controlled environments, and therefore there is no guarantee that they will work fully in all scenarios. It is essential to check the configurations and customizations of the environment where they will be applied to ensure their proper functioning. We thank you for your understanding.

CONTENTS

GREETINGS!

Hello, dear reader!

Welcome to your ultimate journey to master **Flask**, one of the most efficient and versatile frameworks for web development with **Python**. If you've come this far, it's because you recognize the value of learning a powerful tool, capable of transforming ideas into robust, scalable applications ready for the real world.

In **2025**, the demand for Python developers continues to rise, and **Flask** remains a strategic choice for those looking for flexibility, performance and ease in building **APIs and web applications**. With large companies and startups increasingly investing in solutions based on microframeworks, mastering Flask is an essential competitive differentiator for any technology professional.

This book, **"LEARN FLASK: From Fundamentals to Practical Applications"**, was created to offer a clear, didactic and applied path for you to become an expert in the framework. Here, you will learn from Flask fundamentals to building complete, scalable web applications, passing through authentication, database integration, security, performance, WebSockets, cloud deployment and much more.

Each chapter has been carefully structured so that you can read and apply immediately what you learned, building real projects that reflect the needs of the current market. Whether you are a beginner, one Experienced developer looking to upgrade, or someone who wants to create efficient web applications from scratch, this book was made to be yours definitive guide on Flask.

Get ready to transform knowledge into practice, create high-level applications and master one of the most strategic tools in the Python ecosystem.

Happy reading and success in web development with Flask!

ABOUT THE AUTHOR

www.linkedin.com/in/diegoexpertai

Best-Selling Author, Diego Rodrigues is an International Consultant and Writer specializing in Market Intelligence, Technology and Innovation. With 42 international certifications from institutions such as IBM, Google, Microsoft, AWS, Cisco, and Boston University, Ec-Council, Palo Alto and META.

Rodrigues is an expert in Artificial Intelligence, Machine Learning, Data Science, Big Data, Blockchain, Connectivity Technologies, Ethical Hacking and Threat Intelligence.

Since 2003, Rodrigues has developed more than 200 projects for important brands in Brazil, USA and Mexico. In 2024, he consolidates himself as one of the largest new generation authors of technical books in the world, with more than 180 titles published in six languages.

BOOK PRESENTATION

Web development with Python has established itself as one of the most important technological foundations today. Among the various frameworks available, the **Flask** stands out for its lightness, flexibility and ease of use, making it an essential choice for both beginners and experienced developers looking for efficiency in building web applications and APIs.

This book has been carefully crafted to be the most complete and practical guide on Flask, covering everything from fundamentals to advanced applications and deployment strategies. Our goal is to provide a material affordable, up-to-date and highly applicable, allowing you to not only understand the concepts but also implement them efficiently in real projects.

The structure of the book was planned to ensure a fluid progression in learning, combining **theory and practice** in a balanced way.

We start with an introduction **to Flask and the development environment** in **Chapter 1**, addressing the role of the framework in the Python ecosystem, its installation and initial configuration. In **Chapter 2**, we explored the basic structure of a Flask application, including how routes, views and HTTP methods work.

In Chapter **3**, we present the Jinja2 templating system, allowing the creation of dynamic interfaces. Already in **Chapter 4**, we discussed the handling of forms and HTTP requests, a fundamental aspect for any interactive application.

Chapter 5 brings integration with **databases using**

SQLAlchemy, teaching everything from modeling to CRUD operations. In **Chapter 6**, we enter the universe of **APIs REST**, explaining how to build efficient endpoints and test requests using tools like Postman and cURL.

In the second part of the book, we focus on **building complete web applications**. THE **Chapter 7** deals with authentication and access control, covering login, logout and password security. In **Chapter 8**, we discussed **middleware and security**, exploring how to protect applications against common attacks.

In Chapter **9**, we teach **work with uploads and file manipulation**, while the **Chapter 10** explore applications in **real time with WebSockets**, creating a dynamic chat with Flask-SocketIO.

The third part of the book delves into **advanced applications**. In **Chapter 11**, we address **automated tests**, teaching how to ensure code quality. **Chapter 12** focus on **deploy**, demonstrating how to publish Flask applications to services like Heroku, Render, and VPS servers.

No **Chapter 13**, we explore **integration with other technologies**, such as Redis and Celery for asynchronous tasks. In **Chapter 14**, we explain **OAuth and JWT authentication**, fundamental for access control in secure APIs.

Chapter 15 brings an innovative look at **integration between Flask and artificial intelligence**, showing how to build a chatbot and use machine learning within web applications.

In the last part of the book, we build a **complete project** step by step. In Chapter **16**, we define the scope of the project, in **Chapter 17**, we structure the backend and in Chapter **18**, we develop the API services.

In Chapter **19**, we integrated a dynamic frontend with **Bootstrap e Jinja2**. No **Chapter 20**, we work in **performance and optimization**, exploiting efficient caching and requests.

Monitoring and logs are fundamental in any application, and in **Chapter 21**, we discussed how to use tools like Sentry for diagnostics and debugging. Node **Chapter 22**, we reinforce the **advanced security**, preventing attacks and controlling permissions.

No **Chapter 23**, we explore **scalability and cloud integration**, ensuring that your application can grow with increased demand. THE **Chapter 24** deals with **code management and maintenance**, with good versioning practices and continuous updates.

Finally, Chapter **25** analyzes the **future of Flask and web development trends**, offering guidance on new technologies and emerging practices in the sector.

This book has been structured to ensure that you **not only learn Flask, but also know how to apply it in a practical and strategic way**. If you want to create efficient web applications and become an expert in the Python ecosystem, this reading will be an essential step on your journey.

Now, it's time to dive into the world of web development with Flask and turn knowledge into practice!

PART 1: FLASK FUNDAMENTALS

In this first part, we will build a solid foundation in **Flask**, ensuring you understand the fundamental concepts before we move on to more complex applications. The goal here is to provide a clear and practical introduction to the framework, preparing you to develop your own web applications and APIs.

We start at **Chapter 1**, presenting Flask and its role in the Python ecosystem. You will learn how to set up the development environment, install Flask, and create your first working project.

In Chapter **2**, we explored the basic structure of a Flask application, covering the organization of files, the functioning of **routes**, **views** and **HTTP methods**. We'll also look at how to serve HTML pages directly from Flask.

In Chapter **3**, we delve into the system of **templates Jinja2**, essential to create **dynamic and reusable interfaces**. Here, you will learn how to render HTML pages and pass variables from the backend to the frontend.

In Chapter **4**, we move on to handling **forms and HTTP requests**, covering the creation of interactive forms, the use of methods **GET e POST**, and techniques for validating input and handling errors.

THE **Chapter 5** introduces **SQLAlchemy**, one of the most powerful tools for managing databases in Flask. Let's explore from **data modeling** to operations **CRUD (Create, Read, Update, Delete)**, ensuring that your application can store and manipulate information efficiently.

No **Chapter 6**, we end this part with one of the most important topics: **APIs REST**. You will learn to create **RESTful endpoints**, manipulate **JSON**, test requests using **Postman e cURL**, and ensure that your API is well structured for consumption by other applications.

With these fundamentals well established, you will be prepared to move on to the next stage of the book, where we will build complete applications and delve deeper into topics such as authentication, security, WebSockets and much more. Let's get started!

CHAPTER 1 – INTRODUCTION TO FLASK AND DEVELOPMENT ENVIRONMENT

Flask is a **microframework web for Python**, designed to be simple and flexible, allowing developers to create web applications and APIs efficiently and quickly. Unlike more robust frameworks, such as Django, which have many built-in features, Flask follows a minimalist approach, offering only the essentials to start a project.

This model makes it highly modular, allowing developers to choose which libraries and extensions they want to integrate, making it ideal for projects that require flexibility. Its simplicity and low learning curve make it one of the most popular choices for anyone looking to build web applications and REST APIs in Python.

In the Python ecosystem, Flask stands out for its compatibility with various libraries and technologies. It can be used to create simple applications, scalable APIs and even integrate artificial intelligence and machine learning into web systems. Technology companies, startups and even large corporations use Flask in their applications due to its lightness and speed of implementation.

The key components that make Flask an excellent choice for web development include:

- **Routing and Views**: Defines how the application responds to different URLs.
- **Jinja2 Template System**: Allows the creation of dynamic pages.

- **Support for RESTful APIs**: Makes it easier to create modern backend services.
- **Extensions and Integration**: Can be integrated with databases, authentication and other advanced tools.

Flask's architecture follows the principle **WSGI (Web Server Gateway Interface)**, which is a standard for developing web applications in Python. It uses the **Tool**, a library that manages HTTP requests and responses, allowing Flask to function efficiently as a web server.

With this introduction to Flask and its importance in the Python ecosystem, the next step is to prepare the development environment to start coding.

Configuring the environment: Installing Flask, Virtualenv and Pipenv

Before starting to develop applications with Flask, it is essential to set up a suitable environment. For this, we use **Python, pip, Virtualenv e Pipenv**, tools that guarantee an isolated and organized environment for the project.

1. Installing Python and the package manager (pip)

The first step is to ensure that the latest version of Python is installed on the system. To check the version of Python and **pip**, the package manager, run the following command:

bash

```
python --version
pip --version
```

If Python is not installed or is out of date, download the latest version from the official website (python.org) and follow the instructions for installation.

2. Creating a virtual environment with Virtualenv

Virtualenv allows you to create an isolated environment for each project, avoiding conflicts between libraries and dependency versions. To install Virtualenv, use pip:

bash

```
pip install virtualenv
```

After installation, create a new directory for the project and initialize a virtual environment inside it:

bash

```
mkdir my_flask_project
cd my_flask_project
virtualenv venv
```

To activate the virtual environment:

Windows:
bash
```
venv\Scripts\activate
```

Linux/Mac:
bash
```
source venv/bin/activate
```

When the virtual environment is activated, the terminal will display a prefix indicating the name of the environment.

3. Using Pipenv for dependency management

Another modern alternative for managing virtual environments and dependencies is **Pipenv**, which combines Virtualenv and pip into a single tool.

To install Pipenv:

bash

```
pip install pipenv
```

Inside the project directory, start a development environment with:

bash

```
pipenv install flask
```

This command automatically creates a virtual environment and installs Flask. To activate it, use:

bash

```
pipenv shell
```

The advantage of Pipenv is the automatic creation of files Pipfile and Pipfile.lock, ensuring efficient control of project dependencies.

With the environment configured, it's time to create the first Flask application.

Creating your first Flask app

Now that the environment is ready, you can create a basic Flask application. To do this, a file app.py must be created in the project directory.

Open the file and insert the following code:

python

```
from flask import Flask
```

```python
app = Flask(__name__)


@app.route("/")
def home():
    return "Hello, Flask!"


if __name__ == "__main__":
    app.run(debug=True)
```

The code above initializes a Flask application and sets a **main route ("/")** which returns a message to the user.

Explaining the code:

1. **Flask import**: Application is based on class Flask, which manages requests and responses.
2. **Application creation**: app = Flask(__name__) initializes a Flask instance.
3. **Route definition**: The decorator @app.route("/") defines the URL that the function home() will respond.
4. **Server execution**:O app.run(debug=True) starts the Flask server and allows you to view changes in real time.

To run the application, use the command:

bash

```bash
python app.py
```

The terminal will display output similar to this:

csharp

* Running on http://127.0.0.1:5000/ (Press CTRL+C to quit)

Access the browser and type http://127.0.0.1:5000/. The page will display the message **"Hello, Flask!"**, confirming that the server is running correctly.

Project structure

After creating the application, the initial Flask project structure will look like this:

csharp

```
my_flask_project/
| — venv/ # Virtual environment
| — app.py # Main application file
| — Pipfile # Dependency management (if using Pipenv)
| — Pipfile.lock # Lock dependencies (if using Pipenv)
```

This organization makes it easier to expand the project with new features.

Configuring environment variables

To avoid the need to modify code when defining sensitive settings, such as API keys or Flask settings, you can use environment variables.

On Linux and macOS, export the variable with:

bash

```
export FLASK_APP=app.py
export FLASK_ENV=development
```

No Windows, utilize:

bash

```
set FLASK_APP=app.py
set FLASK_ENV=development
```

With this configuration, it is possible to start the application just with:

bash

```
flask run
```

This command offers the same functionality as python app.py, but allows for more efficient management of the Flask application.

With this, the basis for web development with Flask is established, allowing us to move towards structuring the application and creating more complex routes.

CHAPTER 2 – BASIC STRUCTURE OF A FLASK APPLICATION

Understanding the file structure

Flask allows you to build web applications progressively, starting with a simple structure and evolving according to the complexity of the project. Organizing files and directories correctly is essential to ensure maintainability and scalability.

A Flask application can be started with a single Python file, but as it grows, modularization becomes critical. Well-structured projects follow an organization based on specific directories for routes, database models, templates and static files.

The minimum structure for a Flask project can be started with the following format:

csharp

```
my_flask_project/
 |── venv/ # Virtual environment (if using)
 |── app.py # Flask application main file
 |── templates/ # Directory for HTML templates
 |  ├── index.html # Template example
 |── static/ # Directory for static files (CSS, JS, images)
 |── requirements.txt # List of project dependencies
 |── instance/ # Environment-specific settings
 |── config.py # General application settings
```

Each element plays a specific role. The directory templates/ contains HTML files that will be dynamically rendered by Flask. The directory static/ stores files such as images, stylesheets, and JavaScript scripts. THE requirements.txt lists the libraries used in the project, allowing replication of the environment. The directory instance/ may contain custom settings that should not be included in the main repository.

The separation between app.py and config.py allows the centralization of configurations, facilitating code maintenance. Larger projects use the structure **Blueprints**, allowing different parts of the code to be modularized, but before reaching that level, it is essential to understand how the logic of routes and views works.

Routes, Views and HTTP Methods

The concept of **lottery** in Flask defines how a specific URL responds to a request. Each route is linked to a function that processes the request and returns content. Flask uses the decorator @app.route() to associate a URL with a function.

python

```python
from flask import Flask


app = Flask(__name__)


@app.route("/")
def home():
    return "Welcome to Flask!"


if __name__ == "__main__":
```

```
app.run(debug=True)
```

The decorator @app.route("/") defines the application's main route, associating it with the function home(), which returns a string as a response. The server is started by calling app.run(debug=True), enabling debug mode to enable automatic updates during development.

In addition to the GET method, which is the default, it is possible to define routes that accept different HTTP methods. The following example shows how to create a route that accepts both GET and POST.

python

```
from flask import request


@app.route("/submit", methods=["GET", "POST"])
def submit():
    if request.method == "POST":
        return "Data submitted successfully!"
    return "Submit your data using POST."
```

Flask uses the object request to access information sent by the customer. In the code above, the function checks whether the HTTP method used was POST before returning the corresponding response.

When building more advanced applications, it is common to structure routes in an organized way, grouping functionalities into separate modules. An example of a more modularized structure can be implemented with **Blueprints**, which allow you to divide the application into independent parts.

python

```python
from flask import Blueprint


user_routes = Blueprint("user_routes", __name__)


@user_routes.route("/profile")
def profile():
    return "User Profile Page"
```

O Blueprint user_routes can be registered in the main application, making code organization more efficient.

Serving HTML pages with Flask

Flask applications are not limited to responding with text only. Integration with HTML templates allows the framework to generate dynamic pages. Flask uses the **motor de templates Jinja2**, which makes it possible to include variables and logic within HTML files.

To serve an HTML page, you need to use the function render_template(), which searches for a file within the directory templates/.

python

```python
from flask import Flask, render_template


app = Flask(__name__)


@app.route("/")
def home():
```

```
return render_template("index.html")
```

The file index.html must be saved within the directory templates/ and can contain dynamic content using Jinja2 syntax.

html

```html
<!DOCTYPE html>
<html>
<head>
    <title>Flask Web Page</title>
</head>
<body>
    <h1>Welcome to Flask!</h1>
</body>
</html>
```

The integration between Flask and HTML allows the creation of complete applications, including features such as interactive forms and consumption of external APIs. The template structure can be enhanced with layout inheritance, where a base file defines common elements and specific pages fill the necessary spaces.

The file base.html can contain a default layout for all pages in the project.

html

```html
<!DOCTYPE html>
<html>
```

```
<head>
    <title>{% block title %}Flask App{% endblock %}</title>
</head>
<body>
    <header>
        <h1>My Flask App</h1>
    </header>
    <main>
        {% block content %}{% endblock %}
    </main>
</body>
</html>
```

A page index.html can inherit this structure and define specific content.

html
```
{% extends "base.html" %}


{% block title %}Home{% endblock %}


{% block content %}
    <p>Welcome to the homepage!</p>
{% endblock %}
```

With this approach, all application pages can reuse the structure defined in the base template, reducing code duplication and facilitating project maintenance.

Flask also allows the use of static files such as CSS stylesheets and JavaScript scripts. The directory static/ stores these files, and they can be referenced within HTML templates using url_for().

html

```html
<link rel="stylesheet" type="text/css" href="{{ url_for('static', filename='style.css') }}">
```

To load images, the same approach can be used.

html

```html
<img src="{{ url_for('static', filename='images/logo.png') }}" alt="Logo">
```

The proper organization of templates and static files allows Flask to be used to develop from simple web applications to complete systems integrated with databases and APIs.

By understanding the basic structure of a Flask project, including file organization, route creation and integration with templates, application development becomes more efficient. The next step involves implementing dynamic functionality, including forms and HTTP request handling.

CHAPTER 3 – WORKING WITH TEMPLATES IN FLASK

Introduction to Jinja2 and dynamic templates

Flask uses the template engine **Jinja2**, which allows you to create dynamic pages integrated into the backend. A template is an HTML file containing variables and control structures to dynamically display content.

Templates allow Flask applications to be more flexible and reusable, as they avoid the need to write static HTML within Python code. This makes it possible to separate business logic from presentation, improving project organization and facilitating maintenance.

Jinja2 allows the inclusion of variables, loops and conditions within HTML files. The syntax is intuitive and uses **two double keys** {{ }} for displaying variables and **keys with percentage** {% %} for flow control commands.

A basic template structure can contain a dynamic title and a personalized greeting.

html

```
<!DOCTYPE html>

<html>

<head>

    <title>{{ title }}</title>

</head>

<body>
```

```
   <h1>Hello, {{ user }}!</h1>
</body>
</html>
```

The file can be saved in the directory templates/ and rendered by Flask using the function render_template().

python

```python
from flask import Flask, render_template


app = Flask(__name__)


@app.route("/")
def home():
    return render_template("index.html", title="Welcome",
user="John Doe")


if __name__ == "__main__":
    app.run(debug=True)
```

The variable title is used within the tag <title> and user inside the <h1>. Flask replaces these variables with the values passed into the function render_template(), making the page dynamic.

Using templates allows you to create **reusable layouts** and apply **logic within HTML**, such as conditional structures and loops.

Rendering HTML pages

Flask loads templates from the directory templates/. The

function render_template() locates the corresponding HTML file and inserts the values of the variables defined in the backend.

Templates can be rendered directly in HTTP responses. A file about.html saved in directory templates/ can be loaded by route /about.

python

```python
@app.route("/about")
def about():
    return render_template("about.html")
```

The template structure can be expanded to include **dynamic content** using **conditionals and loops**.

A conditional if in Jinja2 allows you to change the display based on variable values.

html

```html
{% if user %}
    <h1>Welcome, {{ user }}!</h1>
{% else %}
    <h1>Welcome, Guest!</h1>
{% endif %}
```

If the variable user is set, the custom greeting will be displayed. Otherwise, "Welcome, Guest!" will be displayed.

The loops for allow you to iterate over lists and display content dynamically.

html

```html
<ul>
```

```
{% for item in items %}
    <li>{{ item }}</li>
{% endfor %}
</ul>
```

If the variable items is a list containing ["Apple", "Banana", "Cherry"], the output will be an HTML list with these elements.

In the backend, the variable can be passed to the template.

python

```
@app.route("/fruits")
def fruits():
    fruit_list = ["Apple", "Banana", "Cherry"]
    return render_template("fruits.html", items=fruit_list)
```

The integration between Flask templates and variables allows you to create dynamic pages, automatically generating content from available data.

Passing variables from Flask to templates

Flask allows passing variables to templates through function render_template(). All variables passed in the function call are available for use in the HTML file.

python

```
@app.route("/profile")
def profile():
    user_data = {
        "name": "Alice",
```

```
    "age": 30,
    "email": "alice@example.com"
}
return render_template("profile.html", user=user_data)
```

In the template, variables can be accessed directly.

html

```html
<h1>User Profile</h1>
<p>Name: {{ user.name }}</p>
<p>Age: {{ user.age }}</p>
<p>Email: {{ user.email }}</p>
```

The lists and dictionaries sent by Flask can be manipulated within templates, allowing the creation of dynamic interfaces.

Template inheritance makes it possible to reuse common layouts across multiple application pages. Jinja2 allows a base template to serve as a framework for other files, avoiding code duplication.

A file base.html can contain elements shared between all pages.

html

```html
<!DOCTYPE html>
<html>
<head>
    <title>{% block title %}My Flask App{% endblock %}</title>
</head>
<body>
```

```html
<header>
    <h1>My Application</h1>
</header>
<main>
    {% block content %}{% endblock %}
</main>
</body>
</html>
```

Pages using this layout can define their specific content by overwriting the **named blocks** ({% block %}).

html
```
{% extends "base.html" %}


{% block title %}Home{% endblock %}


{% block content %}
    <p>Welcome to the homepage!</p>
{% endblock %}
```

O Flask renderiza o template base.html and inserts the content of the blocks defined on each page.

The variables passed by the backend can also be used in HTML and JavaScript attributes.

html
```
<img src="{{ user.profile_picture }}" alt="Profile Picture">
```

Case user.profile_picture contains the URL of an image, it will be loaded correctly in the template.

The use of static files is essential for modern applications. Flask allows you to reference CSS, JavaScript, and image files in the directory static/.

A CSS file can be loaded into a template using url_for().

html

```
<link rel="stylesheet" type="text/css" href="{{ url_for('static', filename='style.css') }}">
```

Flask searches for the file within the directory static/ and returns the correct path to be used in the HTML.

JavaScript scripts can also be loaded using the same approach.

html

```
<script src="{{ url_for('static', filename='script.js') }}"></script>
```

The proper organization of templates, variables and static files allows Flask to be used to create complete applications, with dynamic layouts and content generated from the backend.

By understanding how Jinja2 works and the passage of variables between Flask and templates, web development becomes more efficient and modular.

CHAPTER 4 – HANDLING FORMS AND REQUESTS

Forms are one of the main means of interaction between users and web applications. In Flask, form manipulation can be done manually or using the library **Flask-WTF**, which provides an abstraction layer on top of HTML forms, facilitating data validation and manipulation.

A basic HTML form can be created using the tag <form>, where each input field receives a name which will be used to capture the data sent by the user.

html

```
<form action="/submit" method="POST">
    <label for="name">Name:</label>
    <input type="text" id="name" name="name" required>
    <input type="submit" value="Submit">
</form>
```

The attribute action="/submit" defines the endpoint where the data will be sent, while method="POST" specifies that information must be sent via POST.

In Flask, data capture can be done using the object request.

python

```
from flask import Flask, request, render_template
```

```python
app = Flask(__name__)


@app.route("/")
def index():
    return render_template("form.html")


@app.route("/submit", methods=["POST"])
def submit():
    name = request.form["name"]
    return f"Hello, {name}!"


if __name__ == "__main__":
    app.run(debug=True)
```

The method request.form["name"] accesses the value sent by the form and displays it in the response. If the key does not exist, an error will be generated. To avoid failures, the function request.form.get("name") can be used, as it returns None if the value is not present.

Forms can contain different types of input, such as password fields, check boxes, and drop-down menus.

html

```html
<form action="/register" method="POST">
    <label for="username">Username:</label>
    <input type="text" id="username" name="username"
```

```
    <label for="password">Password:</label>
    <input type="password" id="password" name="password"
required>

    <label for="gender">Gender:</label>
    <select id="gender" name="gender">
        <option value="male">Male</option>
        <option value="female">Female</option>
    </select>

    <input type="submit" value="Register">
</form>
```

Data can be processed in Flask and displayed dynamically.

python

```python
@app.route("/register", methods=["POST"])
def register():
    username = request.form.get("username")
    password = request.form.get("password")
    gender = request.form.get("gender")
    return f"User {username} registered successfully!"
```

The structure allows the form to be expanded as needed,

including features such as file upload, radio buttons and checkboxes.

GET and POST methods

HTTP requests allow applications to interact with web servers. The most used methods are **GET** and **POST**, which define how data is sent and received.

The method **GET** sends data in the URL, being ideal for queries and operations that do not modify the system state.

html

```html
<form action="/search" method="GET">
    <input type="text" name="query" placeholder="Search">
    <input type="submit" value="Search">
</form>
```

Data can be retrieved into Flask using request.args.get().

python

```python
@app.route("/search")
def search():
    query = request.args.get("query")
    return f"Searching for: {query}"
```

The method **POST** sends data in the body of the request, being used for operations that involve data modification.

html

```html
<form action="/login" method="POST">
    <input type="text" name="username" required>
    <input type="password" name="password" required>
```

```
    <input type="submit" value="Login">
</form>
```

Flask recovers data using request.form.get().

python

```python
@app.route("/login", methods=["POST"])
def login():
    username = request.form.get("username")
    password = request.form.get("password")
    return f"User {username} logged in successfully!"
```

Additional methods such as **PUT**, **DELETE** and **PATCH**, are used for specific operations in RESTful APIs.

Input validation and error handling

Validation of data sent by the user is essential to ensure security and integrity. Flask allows manual validation using conditionals or through the extension **Flask-WTF**, which integrates pre-defined validations.

A simple validation can be done by checking whether the fields are filled in correctly.

python

```python
@app.route("/validate", methods=["POST"])
def validate():
    email = request.form.get("email")
    if not email or "@" not in email:
        return "Invalid email address!", 400
```

```
return "Email is valid!"
```

If an invalid email is sent, the response will return the code **400 Bad Request**.

The Flask-WTF library allows for more sophisticated validation control.

python

```
from flask_wtf import FlaskForm

from wtforms import StringField, PasswordField

from wtforms.validators import DataRequired, Email


class LoginForm(FlaskForm):
    email = StringField("Email", validators=[DataRequired(), Email()])
    password = PasswordField("Password", validators=[DataRequired()])
```

Errors can be captured and displayed dynamically in templates.

html

```
{% for field, errors in form.errors.items() %}
    <p>{{ field }}: {{ ", ".join(errors) }}</p>
{% endfor %}
```

Error handling prevents unexpected crashes and improves user experience.

Common mistakes and how to fix them

Error: Key not found in request.form

Error message:

vbnet

KeyError: 'username'

Probable cause: The form did not send the key username or the field is empty.

Solution: Utilize request.form.get("username") to avoid exceptions.

Error: Invalid data type

Error message:

csharp

ValueError: invalid literal for int() with base 10: 'abc'

Probable cause: A numeric field has been assigned a non-numeric value.

Solution: Validate the data before converting it.

python

```
age = request.form.get("age")
if not age.isdigit():
    return "Invalid age input!"
```

Error: CSRF Token Missing

Error message:

r

csrf token missing or incorrect

Probable cause: The form did not include a CSRF token.

Solution: Use Flask-WTF and include {{ form.hidden_tag() }} no template.

Correct handling of forms and requests ensures application security and improves the user experience.

CHAPTER 4 – HANDLING FORMS AND REQUESTS

User interaction with web applications largely depends on form handling. Flask provides full support for capturing, processing, and validating user-submitted data via HTTP requests.

An HTML form can be defined using the tag <form>. The attribute action defines the destination of the sent data, while method specifies how data will be transmitted.

html

```html
<form action="/submit" method="POST">
    <label for="username">Username:</label>
    <input type="text" id="username" name="username" required>

    <label for="email">Email:</label>
    <input type="email" id="email" name="email" required>

    <input type="submit" value="Send">
</form>
```

Flask captures the data submitted by the form through the object request.

python

```python
from flask import Flask, request, render_template


app = Flask(__name__)


@app.route("/")
def index():
    return render_template("form.html")


@app.route("/submit", methods=["POST"])
def submit():
    username = request.form.get("username")
    email = request.form.get("email")
    return f"User {username} with email {email} submitted successfully!"


if __name__ == "__main__":
    app.run(debug=True)
```

THE request.form.get() retrieves the data sent by the form. If the field is not filled, returns None instead of throwing an error.

Forms can contain different types of input, such as checkboxes, radio buttons and selects.

html

```html
<form action="/preferences" method="POST">
    <label for="newsletter">Subscribe to newsletter:</label>
```

```html
    <input type="checkbox" id="newsletter" name="newsletter"
value="yes">


    <label>Choose a color:</label>
    <input type="radio" name="color" value="red"> Red
    <input type="radio" name="color" value="blue"> Blue


    <input type="submit" value="Save">
</form>
```

Flask receives these values in the same way.

python

```python
@app.route("/preferences", methods=["POST"])
def preferences():
    newsletter = request.form.get("newsletter", "no")
    color = request.form.get("color", "none")
    return f"Preferences saved: Newsletter - {newsletter}, Color -
{color}"
```

If no amount is sent to newsletter, the default value "no" will be returned.

GET and POST methods

Forms can be submitted using different HTTP methods.

The method **GET** sends data via URL.

html

```html
<form action="/search" method="GET">
```

```html
    <input type="text" name="query" placeholder="Search">
    <input type="submit" value="Search">
</form>
```

Flask recovers data with request.args.get().

python

```python
@app.route("/search")
def search():
    query = request.args.get("query", "")
    return f"Searching for: {query}"
```

The method **POST** sends the data in the request body, making it invisible in the URL.

html

```html
<form action="/login" method="POST">
    <input type="text" name="username" required>
    <input type="password" name="password" required>
    <input type="submit" value="Login">
</form>
```

Flask captures data with request.form.get().

python

```python
@app.route("/login", methods=["POST"])
def login():
    username = request.form.get("username")
```

```python
password = request.form.get("password")
return f"User {username} logged in successfully!"
```

Additional methods like **PUT**, **PATCH** and **DELETE** are used in REST APIs for specific operations.

Input validation and error handling

Data validation prevents problems such as incorrect or malicious entries.

Flask allows manual validation using conditionals.

python

```python
@app.route("/validate", methods=["POST"])
def validate():
    email = request.form.get("email")
    if not email or "@" not in email:
        return "Invalid email address!", 400
    return "Email is valid!"
```

If an invalid email is entered, the response returns the HTTP code **400 Bad Request**.

The library **Flask-WTF** facilitates form validation and includes CSRF protection.

python

```python
from flask_wtf import FlaskForm
from wtforms import StringField, PasswordField
from wtforms.validators import DataRequired, Email
```

```
class LoginForm(FlaskForm):
    email = StringField("Email", validators=[DataRequired(),
Email()])
    password = PasswordField("Password",
validators=[DataRequired()])
```

Errors can be displayed in templates.

html

```
{% for field, errors in form.errors.items() %}
    <p>{{ field }}: {{ ", ".join(errors) }}</p>
{% endfor %}
```

Common mistakes and how to fix them

Key not found in request.form

Error message:

vbnet

KeyError: 'username'

Probable cause: The form did not send the field username or was sent under another name.

Solution: Utilize request.form.get("username") to avoid exceptions.

Invalid die type

Error message:

csharp

ValueError: invalid literal for int() with base 10: 'abc'

Probable cause: A numeric field has been assigned a non-numeric value.

Solution: Validate input before conversion.

python

```
age = request.form.get("age", "0")
if not age.isdigit():
    return "Invalid age input!"
```

CSRF Token Missing

Error message:

r

csrf token missing or incorrect

Probable cause: The form did not include a CSRF token to protect against attacks.

Solution: Utilize **Flask-WTF** and add {{ form.hidden_tag() }} no template.

The correct handling of forms and requests improves the security and usability of the application. The next step involves integration with databases to store information.

CHAPTER 5 – DATABASE IN FLASK WITH SQLALCHEMY

Introduction to SQLAlchemy and ORM

Flask offers integration with several databases, the **SQLAlchemy** one of the most used libraries for data manipulation. SQLAlchemy is a **Object Relational Mapper (ORM)**, allowing communication with relational databases in a programmatic and structured way.

An ORM converts tables and records in a database into Python objects, enabling manipulations using code instead of direct SQL commands. This approach improves code readability and reduces the likelihood of SQL syntax errors.

SQLAlchemy allows the use of **two main modes**:

- **Core (SQL Expression Language):** Uses direct SQL expressions, offering greater control over queries.
- **ORM (Object Relational Mapper):** Represents tables as Python classes, allowing more intuitive data manipulation.

The ORM approach makes it easy to create, read, update and delete records without having to write SQL queries manually.

Creating and managing databases in Flask

Installing SQLAlchemy can be done using pip.

bash

```
pip install flask-sqlalchemy
```

After installation, SQLAlchemy can be integrated with Flask by configuring the database in the application.

python

```
from flask import Flask
from flask_sqlalchemy import SQLAlchemy

app = Flask(__name__)
app.config["SQLALCHEMY_DATABASE_URI"] = "sqlite:///
database.db"
app.config["SQLALCHEMY_TRACK_MODIFICATIONS"] = False

db = SQLAlchemy(app)
```

The database can be configured using different **database engines**, incluindo SQLite, PostgreSQL e MySQL.

- **SQLite:** sqlite:///database.db
- **PostgreSQL:** postgresql://user:password@localhost/dbname
- **MySQL:** mysql://user:password@localhost/dbname

With the configuration established, the next step is to define data models that will represent tables in the database.

Model Definition

Models represent database tables and are defined as Python classes that inherit from db.Model.

python

```
class User(db.Model):
```

```python
id = db.Column(db.Integer, primary_key=True)

username = db.Column(db.String(80), unique=True,
nullable=False)

email = db.Column(db.String(120), unique=True,
nullable=False)


def __repr__(self):
    return f"<User {self.username}>"
```

Each class attribute represents a **column** of the table.

- id = db.Column(db.Integer, primary_key=True): **Defines the primary key.**
- username = db.Column(db.String(80), unique=True, nullable=False): **Defines a string of up to 80 characters, unique and mandatory.**
- email = db.Column(db.String(120), unique=True, nullable=False): **Defines email as a single and mandatory field.**

The database can be initialized by creating tables with the method db.create_all().

python

```python
with app.app_context():
    db.create_all()
```

The command checks the defined models and creates the tables in the database if they do not already exist.

Basic CRUD Operations

The operations **CRUD (Create, Read, Update, Delete)** represent the essential manipulation of data in a database. SQLAlchemy allows you to perform these operations directly on models.

Creating records

To add new records, objects are instantiated and added to the database session.

python

```
new_user = User(username="john_doe",
email="john@example.com")

db.session.add(new_user)

db.session.commit()
```

The method add() adds the object to the session, and commit() saves changes to the database.

Reading records

Records can be retrieved using ORM queries.

python

```
users = User.query.all() # Returns all users

user = User.query.filter_by(username="john_doe").first() #
Returns a specific user
```

The method all() returns all records, while first() returns the first matching result.

Updating records

Data updating can be done by retrieving a record, modifying its attributes, and committing the changes.

python

```
user = User.query.filter_by(username="john_doe").first()
```

```
if user:
    user.email = "new_email@example.com"
    db.session.commit()
```

The attribute email is modified and the change is saved using commit().

Deleting records

Removing records follows a similar logic to updating.

python

```
user = User.query.filter_by(username="john_doe").first()
if user:
    db.session.delete(user)
    db.session.commit()
```

The method delete() remove the registry and commit() confirms the operation.

Common mistakes and how to fix them

Error: Database was not created

Error message:

pgsql

```
sqlite3.OperationalError: no such table: user
```

Probable cause: The command db.create_all() was not executed before attempting to manipulate the data.

Solution: Make sure to initialize the database before any operations.

python

```
with app.app_context():
    db.create_all()
```

Error: Duplicate key when inserting data

Error message:

pgsql

```
IntegrityError: UNIQUE constraint failed: user.email
```

Probable cause: The field email was defined as unique and the insertion attempt used an existing value.

Solution: Check if the email already exists before entering a new user.

python

```
existing_user =
User.query.filter_by(email="john@example.com").first()
if not existing_user:
    new_user = User(username="john_doe",
email="john@example.com")
    db.session.add(new_user)
    db.session.commit()
```

Error: Update failed because object was not found

Error message:

pgsql

```
AttributeError: 'NoneType' object has no attribute 'email'
```

Probable cause: No users were found in the query.

Solution: Verify that the object exists before trying to modify its attributes.

python

```python
user = User.query.filter_by(username="john_doe").first()
if user:
    user.email = "new_email@example.com"
    db.session.commit()
```

Flask's integration with SQLAlchemy allows you to manipulate databases in a structured and efficient way. Defining templates simplifies table creation, and CRUD operations give you complete control over stored data.

CHAPTER 6 – FLASK AND REST APIS

Creating RESTful endpoints with Flask

As **APIs REST (Representational State Transfer)** They are one of the most used standards for communication between applications. Flask allows you to build APIs in an efficient and scalable way, using routes, HTTP methods and data manipulation in **JSON**.

One **endpoint RESTful** is a specific URL that responds to an HTTP request with a certain behavior. Each endpoint can support different HTTP methods, such as:

- **GET**: Retrieves information
- **POST**: Sends data to the server
- **PUT**: Update records
- **DELETE**: Removes resources

In Flask, a basic endpoint can be defined using the decorator @app.route().

python

```
from flask import Flask, jsonify


app = Flask(__name__)


@app.route("/api/status", methods=["GET"])
def status():
    return jsonify({"status": "API is running"})
```

```
if __name__ == "__main__":

    app.run(debug=True)
```

The method jsonify() converts a Python dictionary into a JSON response, ensuring that the Content-Type of the answer is application/json.

Creating REST APIs in Flask can be organized using **Blueprints**, facilitating code modularization.

python

```
from flask import Blueprint, jsonify


api = Blueprint("api", __name__)


@api.route("/info", methods=["GET"])
def info():
    return jsonify({"framework": "Flask", "version": "2.1.0"})
```

THE **Blueprint** can be registered in the main application.

python

```
app.register_blueprint(api, url_prefix="/api")
```

This way, the API endpoints are organized under the URL /api/.

JSON and HTTP response handling

The format **JSON (JavaScript Object Notation)** It is widely used to exchange information between client and server. In Flask, the jsonify() automatically converts dictionaries to JSON, as well as setting the correct response header.

python

```python
@app.route("/user/<int:user_id>", methods=["GET"])
def get_user(user_id):
    user = {"id": user_id, "name": "John Doe", "email":
"john@example.com"}
    return jsonify(user)
```

Flask allows you to send **different HTTP status codes** using the second argument of the function jsonify().

python

```python
@app.route("/error", methods=["GET"])
def error():
    return jsonify({"error": "Invalid request"}), 400
```

The most common status codes include:

- **200 OK**: Response successful
- **201 Created**: Resource created successfully
- **400 Bad Request**: Invalid request
- **404 Not Found**: Resource not found
- **500 Internal Server Error**: Internal server error

Requests sent to Flask may contain **JSON data in the request body**, accessible by the object request.

python

```python
from flask import request
```

```
@app.route("/create_user", methods=["POST"])
def create_user():
    data = request.get_json()
    return jsonify({"message": f"User {data['name']} created
successfully!"}), 201
```

The function get_json() extracts the JSON content of the request and allows you to manipulate the data in the backend.

Testing APIs with Postman and cURL

Validating an API is essential to ensure its correct functioning. Tools like **Postman** and **cURL** allow you to test endpoints without the need for a full frontend.

THE **Postman** provides a graphical interface for sending HTTP requests. To test an endpoint:

1. Open Postman and select the method **GET**.
2. Enter the URL http://127.0.0.1:5000/api/status.
3. Click **Send** to view the JSON response.

Requests **POST** can be tested by sending a JSON body in the tab **Body**.

json

```
{
    "name": "Alice",
    "email": "alice@example.com"
}
```

THE **cURL** is a command-line tool that allows you to test APIs directly from the terminal.

To send a request **GET**:

bash

```
curl -X GET http://127.0.0.1:5000/api/status
```

To send data using **POST**:

bash

```
curl -X POST http://127.0.0.1:5000/create_user -H "Content-Type: application/json" -d '{"name": "Alice"}'
```

The API response will be returned in the terminal.

Common mistakes and how to fix them

Error: Failed to process JSON in the request

Error message:

csharp

```
TypeError: 'NoneType' object is not subscriptable
```

Probable cause: The request body does not contain JSON or the header Content-Type was not set correctly.

Solution: Make sure the data is being sent in JSON format.

python

```
data = request.get_json()
if not data:
    return jsonify({"error": "Missing JSON data"}), 400
```

The correct header must be used when sending data over the

cURL or Postman.

bash

-H "Content-Type: application/json"

Error: Route not found

Error message:

pgsql

404 Not Found: The requested URL was not found on the server.

Probable cause: The endpoint was not defined correctly or the request URL is wrong.

Solution: Confirm that the route is registered correctly.

python

```python
@app.route("/data", methods=["GET"])
def get_data():
    return jsonify({"message": "Success"})
```

The request must be made to /data and not /info.

Error: HTTP method not allowed

Error message:

405 Method Not Allowed

Probable cause: The request method does not match what the API accepts.

Solution: Check which methods are allowed for the endpoint.

python

```python
@app.route("/update", methods=["POST"])
```

```
def update():
    return jsonify({"message": "Updated successfully"})
```

If a **GET** is sent to /update, the error **405** will be generated. The correct request must be made using **POST**.

Flask allows you to build efficient REST APIs using routes, JSON manipulation, and integration with testing tools like Postman and cURL.

PART 2: BUILDING WEB APPLICATIONS

Creating web applications with Flask goes beyond the basic structure of routes and templates. The robustness and security of a system depend on features such as **authentication, access control, security against attacks, file manipulation and real-time communication**. This part of the book focuses on these essential aspects to transform a simple Flask application into a complete and functional system.

The first step to ensuring user security and privacy is **authentication and access control**. No **Chapter 7**, it will be explained how to create **login and logout systems**, store passwords securely using **Flask-Bcrypt** and manage **user sessions with Flask-Login**. These practices are essential for applications that require login to access certain areas or functionalities.

In addition to authentication, it is essential to implement **additional security layers** to protect the application against common attacks. THE **Chapter 8** will address **middleware for security and logging**, protection against **CSRF e XSS**, in addition to good practices that avoid known vulnerabilities in web development. Proper use of middleware allows certain security checks and actions to be applied before requests reach the application routes.

THE **Chapter 9** focuses on **file handling and uploads**, a common feature in applications that deal with sending images, documents and other types of data. In addition to learning how to accept and store files, protection against **malicious files and upload attacks**, ensuring that only safe content is processed by the server.

Finally, the **Chapter 10** explores Flask integration with **WebSockets** to create **real-time applications**. This technology allows bidirectional communication between client and server without the need for repetitive requests, being widely used for **real-time chats, notifications and dynamic interface updates**. To library **Flask-SocketIO** will be used to demonstrate how to build a **dynamic chat** and how to integrate this functionality with **interactive frontend**.

This part of the book teaches you how to transform a basic Flask application into a complete and secure system, covering everything from authentication and security to real-time communication. Building modern web applications requires mastery of these tools, making them essential for any Flask developer.

CHAPTER 7 – AUTHENTICATION AND ACCESS CONTROL

Creating login and logout systems

Authentication is one of the pillars of security in web applications. It ensures that only authorized users have access to certain system functionalities. Flask supports implementing login and logout systems using sessions and password hashing.

Authentication can be done in several ways, including **session cookies, JWT and OAuth tokens**. The traditional method uses **sessions** to store user information after a successful login.

Implementing a basic login system in Flask involves three main steps:

1. **Creation of the user database**
2. **Credential verification and secure password storage**
3. **Session management to keep users authenticated**

The user base can be represented using **Flask-SQLAlchemy**.

python

```
from flask import Flask

from flask_sqlalchemy import SQLAlchemy


app = Flask(__name__)

app.config["SQLALCHEMY_DATABASE_URI"] = "sqlite:///users.db"

app.config["SQLALCHEMY_TRACK_MODIFICATIONS"] = False
```

```
db = SQLAlchemy(app)


class User(db.Model):
    id = db.Column(db.Integer, primary_key=True)
    username = db.Column(db.String(80), unique=True,
nullable=False)
    password_hash = db.Column(db.String(128), nullable=False)


    def __repr__(self):
        return f"<User {self.username}>"


with app.app_context():
    db.create_all()
```

Users will be stored in the database and their passwords will need to be hashed before being saved.

Password hashing with Flask-Bcrypt

THE **Flask-Bcrypt** is an extension that allows secure storage of passwords. THE **hashing** converts the password into an irreversible format, preventing passwords from being stored in plain text.

Installation can be done with pip.

bash

```
pip install flask-bcrypt
```

The library can be integrated into the application to manage passwords securely.

python

```python
from flask_bcrypt import Bcrypt


bcrypt = Bcrypt(app)


def hash_password(password):
    return
bcrypt.generate_password_hash(password).decode("utf-8")


def check_password(password, hashed_password):
    return bcrypt.check_password_hash(hashed_password,
password)
```

When registering a new user, the password will be stored securely.

python

```python
hashed_password = hash_password("my_secure_password")
new_user = User(username="john_doe",
password_hash=hashed_password)
db.session.add(new_user)
db.session.commit()
```

When authenticating a user, the provided password will be compared to the stored hash.

python

```python
user = User.query.filter_by(username="john_doe").first()
if user and check_password("my_secure_password",
```

```
user.password_hash):
    print("Login successful")
else:
    print("Invalid credentials")
```

This approach prevents passwords from being recovered in the event of a data leak, as the **hash cannot be reverted to the original password**.

Sessions and authentication with Flask-Login

THE **Flask-Login** simplifies user session management by providing functionality for login, logout and access control.

Installation can be done with pip.

bash

```
pip install flask-login
```

The extension must be configured in the application.

python

```
from flask_login import LoginManager, UserMixin, login_user,
logout_user, login_required, current_user


login_manager = LoginManager(app)
login_manager.login_view = "login"


class User(db.Model, UserMixin):
    id = db.Column(db.Integer, primary_key=True)
    username = db.Column(db.String(80), unique=True,
nullable=False)
```

```
password_hash = db.Column(db.String(128), nullable=False)


@login_manager.user_loader
def load_user(user_id):
    return User.query.get(int(user_id))
```

THE **UserMixin** provides methods that help Flask-Login recognize the authenticated user. The method load_user() loads a user based on the ID stored in the session.

The login route verifies the credentials and starts the user session.

python

```
from flask import request, redirect, url_for
from flask_login import login_user


@app.route("/login", methods=["GET", "POST"])
def login():
    if request.method == "POST":
        username = request.form.get("username")
        password = request.form.get("password")
        user = User.query.filter_by(username=username).first()
        if user and check_password(password,
user.password_hash):
            login_user(user)
            return redirect(url_for("dashboard"))
    return render_template("login.html")
```

The protected route requires authentication to access.

python

```python
@app.route("/dashboard")
@login_required
def dashboard():
    return f"Welcome, {current_user.username}!"
```

The decorator @login_required prevents unauthenticated users from accessing the page.

Logout removes the user from the session.

python

```python
from flask_login import logout_user

@app.route("/logout")
@login_required
def logout():
    logout_user()
    return redirect(url_for("login"))
```

THE **Flask-Login** stores the user session in a secure session cookie, ensuring that only authenticated users have access to restricted areas.

Frontend Implementation for Login

The login form can be created with HTML.

html

```html
<form action="/login" method="POST">
    <label for="username">Username:</label>
    <input type="text" name="username" required>

    <label for="password">Password:</label>
    <input type="password" name="password" required>

    <input type="submit" value="Login">
</form>
```

The system can be expanded to include **remember user**, **password recovery** and **role-based authorization**.

Common errors and how to resolve them

Error: AttributeError: 'NoneType' object has no attribute 'password_hash'

Cause: The user was not found in the database.

Solution: Check if user and None before accessing password_hash.

python

```python
user = User.query.filter_by(username=username).first()
if user and check_password(password, user.password_hash):
    login_user(user)
else:
    return "Invalid credentials"
```

Error: LoginManager not initialized

STUDIOD21 SMART TECH CONTENT

Cause: THE LoginManager was not configured correctly.

Solution: Be sure to call login_manager.init_app(app) after setting LoginManager(app).

Error: Unauthorized: You must be logged in to access this page

Cause: Attempt to access a protected route without authentication.

Solution: The user must be redirected to the login page before accessing restricted areas.

python

```
login_manager.login_view = "login"
```

Implementing authentication in Flask ensures that users can access the system securely.

CHAPTER 8 – MIDDLEWARE AND SECURITY IN FLASK APPLICATIONS

Implementing middleware for security and logging

Middleware is a layer of code executed before or after HTTP requests reach the application routes. It allows you to add features like **logging, authentication, permissions checking and attack protection**. In Flask, middleware can be implemented using **before_request and after_request functions** or by creating extensions.

A secure application needs to monitor requests to detect suspicious patterns, record user activities and prevent unauthorized access. A basic middleware for **request logging** can be implemented using the function before_request.

python

```
from flask import Flask, request

import logging


app = Flask(__name__)


logging.basicConfig(filename="access.log", level=logging.INFO,
format="%(asctime)s - %(message)s")


@app.before_request
```

```python
def log_request():
    logging.info(f"Request: {request.method} {request.url} - IP: {request.remote_addr}")


@app.route("/")
def home():
    return "Welcome to Flask Security!"


if __name__ == "__main__":
    app.run(debug=True)
```

The function before_request is executed before each request, recording the HTTP method, the URL accessed and the user's IP address. THE logging allows you to store this information in a log file for auditing and detecting suspicious activity.

The middleware can also be used to **block suspicious IPs**.

python

```python
BLOCKED_IPS = ["192.168.1.10"]


@app.before_request
def block_suspicious_ips():
    if request.remote_addr in BLOCKED_IPS:
        return "Access denied", 403
```

This approach prevents IP addresses known for malicious behavior from accessing the application.

The function after_request can be used for **modify responses before sending them to the client**.

python

```
@app.after_request
def add_security_headers(response):
    response.headers["X-Frame-Options"] = "DENY"
    response.headers["X-Content-Type-Options"] = "nosniff"
    response.headers["Referrer-Policy"] = "no-referrer"
    return response
```

These headers increase application security by preventing attacks such as **clickjacking and content manipulation**.

Protection against CSRF and XSS attacks

The attacks **Cross-Site Request Forgery (CSRF)** and **Cross-Site Scripting (XSS)** are common threats in web applications.

CSRF occurs when an attacker exploits a user's authenticated session to perform unwanted actions. THE **Flask-WTF** provides protection against this type of attack by adding CSRF tokens to requests.

Installation can be done with pip.

bash

```
pip install flask-wtf
```

CSRF protection is enabled by configuring the secret key and adding CSRFProtect in the application.

python

```
from flask_wtf.csrf import CSRFProtect
```

```
app.config["SECRET_KEY"] = "your_secret_key"
csrf = CSRFProtect(app)
```

All forms must include a **token CSRF** for validation.

html

```html
<form action="/submit" method="POST">
    {{ csrf_token() }}
    <input type="text" name="name">
    <input type="submit" value="Send">
</form>
```

This prevents an attacker from sending forged requests using the user's session without authorization.

THE **XSS** occurs when an attacker injects malicious JavaScript code into the application, exploiting flaws in data input sanitization. The best practice to avoid XSS is **sanitize and escape all dynamic content** before displaying it in the frontend.

Jinja2, used by Flask, already automatically escapes the values rendered in templates.

html

```html
<p>{{ user_input }}</p>
```

However, if the output must contain valid HTML, the filter |safe can be used with caution.

html

```html
<p>{{ user_input | safe }}</p>
```

Se user_input contain `<script>alert('XSS')</script>`, the version without safe will display the string as text, while the version with safe will execute JavaScript code in the browser, allowing an XSS attack.

One approach to preventing XSS attacks is to validate and sanitize input using libraries such as **Bleach**.

Installation can be done with pip.

bash

```
pip install bleach
```

Bleach removes or neutralizes malicious elements from user input.

python

```
import bleach


@app.route("/comment", methods=["POST"])
def comment():
    raw_comment = request.form.get("comment")
    sanitized_comment = bleach.clean(raw_comment)
    return f"Comment: {sanitized_comment}"
```

This prevents users from inserting malicious scripts into the application's comments field.

Good security practices at Flask

The security of a Flask application involves several layers of protection. Some good practices include:

- **Always use HTTPS** to prevent data interception.
- **Disable DEBUG mode in production**, as it may expose sensitive information.
- **Limit login attempts** to prevent brute force attacks.
- **Store passwords securely** using hashing.
- **Validate all user input** before processing them.
- **Utilizar Content Security Policy (CSP)** to restrict loading of external scripts.

The configuration of **HTTPS** can be applied using a reverse proxy like **Nginx** or enabling TLS on the Flask server.

The mode **DEBUG** must be disabled before deploying the application.

python

```python
if __name__ == "__main__":
    app.run(debug=False)
```

Limiting login attempts can be implemented with **Flask-Limiter** to block multiple attempts in a short period.

Installation can be done with pip.

bash

```bash
pip install flask-limiter
```

The setting prevents a user from trying to authenticate multiple times in a row.

python

```python
from flask_limiter import Limiter
from flask_limiter.util import get_remote_address
```

```
limiter = Limiter(app, key_func=get_remote_address)
```

```
@app.route("/login", methods=["POST"])
@limiter.limit("5 per minute")
def login():
    return "Login attempt"
```

This rule restricts the number of login attempts to **5 per minute** by IP address.

The implementation of **Content Security Policy (CSP)** prevents the execution of malicious scripts loaded from external domains.

python

```
@app.after_request
def add_security_headers(response):
    response.headers["Content-Security-Policy"] = "default-src 'self'"
    return response
```

This ensures that only scripts hosted on the application's own domain are executed.

Security in REST APIs

The same security practices applied to web applications should be used in APIs.

Key points include:

- **Authentication with JWT tokens** to prevent misuse of sessions.
- **Protection against CORS (Cross-Origin Resource Sharing)** restricting which domains can access the API.
- **Request rate limiting** to avoid server overload.

The implementation of **CORS** can be done using Flask-CORS.

Installation can be done with pip.

bash

```
pip install flask-cors
```

The configuration only allows requests from authorized domains.

python

```
from flask_cors import CORS


CORS(app, resources={r"/api/*": {"origins": "https://
trusteddomain.com"}})
```

This prevents scripts from other sites from consuming API resources without authorization.

The security of a Flask application must be designed from the beginning, using middleware for monitoring, protection against CSRF and XSS attacks, and good configuration practices.

CHAPTER 9 – UPLOADING AND MANIPULATING FILES IN FLASK

How to accept and validate file uploads

Web applications often require file upload functionality, whether to store profile images, documents or any other type of user-uploaded data. Flask provides support for handling uploads using the request.files, allowing files to be sent and processed efficiently.

The first step to implementing file upload is to create an HTML form that allows the user to select and upload a file.

html

```
<form action="/upload" method="POST" enctype="multipart/form-data">
    <label for="file">Choose a file:</label>
    <input type="file" name="file" required>
    <input type="submit" value="Upload">
</form>
```

The attribute enctype="multipart/form-data" It is essential for the browser to send the file correctly to the server.

On the backend, Flask receives the file through the object request.files.

python

from flask import Flask, request

```python
app = Flask(__name__)

@app.route("/upload", methods=["POST"])
def upload_file():
    if "file" not in request.files:
        return "No file part", 400

    file = request.files["file"]
    if file.filename == "":
        return "No selected file", 400

    file.save(f"./uploads/{file.filename}")
    return f"File {file.filename} uploaded successfully!"

if __name__ == "__main__":
    app.run(debug=True)
```

The code checks whether a file was uploaded and whether it has a valid name before storing it in the directory uploads/.

To avoid failures when saving files, the destination directory must exist before the save attempt.

python

import them

```
UPLOAD_FOLDER = "./uploads"
os.makedirs(UPLOAD_FOLDER, exist_ok=True)
```

```
app.config["UPLOAD_FOLDER"] = UPLOAD_FOLDER
```

This ensures that Flask can store files without errors.

Image storage and manipulation

Flask allows file manipulation after upload, including **resizing, format conversion and compression of images**. To library **Pillow** It is widely used to process images in Python.

Installation can be done with pip.

bash

```
pip install pillow
```

With the library installed, an image can be opened and resized before saving.

python

```
from PIL import Image
```

```
@app.route("/upload_image", methods=["POST"])
def upload_image():
    if "file" not in request.files:
        return "No file part", 400
```

```python
file = request.files["file"]
if file.filename == "":
    return "No selected file", 400


img = Image.open(file)
img = img.resize((300, 300)) # Redimensiona para 300x300 pixels


img.save(os.path.join(app.config["UPLOAD_FOLDER"], file.filename))
return f"Image {file.filename} uploaded and resized successfully!"
```

This code resizes the image before storing it on the server, reducing space consumption and improving application performance.

Other operations can be performed, such as format conversion.

python

```python
img.convert("L").save(os.path.join(app.config["UPLOAD_FOLDER"], "grayscale_" + file.filename))
```

This generates a grayscale version of the image.

Protection against malicious uploads

Uploading files can pose a security risk if there is no proper validation. Malicious files can be sent to exploit vulnerabilities on the server.

The first step to ensuring security is **limit allowed file types**.

python

```
ALLOWED_EXTENSIONS = {"png", "jpg", "jpeg", "gif", "pdf"}


def allowed_file(filename):
    return "." in filename and filename.rsplit(".", 1)[1].lower() in ALLOWED_EXTENSIONS
```

Before processing the file, you need to check whether the extension is allowed.

python

```
if not allowed_file(file.filename):
    return "Invalid file type", 400
```

Furthermore, **avoid malicious file names** is essential. The library tool.utils provides the function secure_filename() to prevent attacks based on file name manipulation.

Installation can be done with pip.

bash

```
pip install tool
```

The function secure_filename() normalizes the file name by removing special characters.

python

```
from werkzeug.utils import secure_filename
```

```
filename = secure_filename(file.filename)
file.save(os.path.join(app.config["UPLOAD_FOLDER"], filename))
```

This prevents a user from uploading a file with a name like "../../ etc/passwd", trying to overwrite system files.

Another common threat is disguised files, where an attacker sends a file .jpg which actually contains malicious code. One way to mitigate this risk is **validate file signature** instead of just relying on the extension.

With **Pillow**, checking the actual image format can be done.

python

```
try:
    img = Image.open(file)
    img.verify()
except Exception:
    return "Invalid image file", 400
```

This prevents invalid files from being accepted.

Common mistakes and how to fix them

Error: No files were sent

Error message:

yaml

```
No file part
```

Probable cause: The form did not upload a file or the upload field was left blank.

Solution: Check if the field file exists in the request.

python

```
if "file" not in request.files:
    return "No file part", 400
```

Error: File type not allowed

Error message:

bash

```
Invalid file type
```

Probable cause: The uploaded file has an extension that is not allowed.

Solution: Define a list of valid extensions and check the extension before processing the file.

python

```
ALLOWED_EXTENSIONS = {"png", "jpg", "jpeg", "gif", "pdf"}
if not allowed_file(file.filename):
    return "Invalid file type", 400
```

Error: Destination path does not exist

Error message:

yaml

```
FileNotFoundError: [Errno 2] No such file or directory
```

Probable cause: The storage directory was not created before saving the file.

Solution: Create the directory uploads/ if it doesn't exist.

python

```python
UPLOAD_FOLDER = "./uploads"
os.makedirs(UPLOAD_FOLDER, exist_ok=True)
```

Flask's file upload implementation allows you to accept, validate, and store files securely. Image manipulation can be used to optimize and process files uploaded by users.

CHAPTER 10 – FLASK WITH WEBSOCKETS AND REAL-TIME APPLICATIONS

Introduction to WebSockets on Flask

Real-time communication is essential for modern applications, allowing instant interactivity without the need to reload pages or make multiple requests to the server. The protocol **WebSocket** enables a persistent connection between client and server, allowing **sending and receiving two-way messages** no noticeable latency.

Unlike traditional HTTP requests, where each request requires an immediate response, WebSockets **maintain an open channel of communication**, allowing both the client and server to send messages at any time.

Flask supports WebSockets through the extension **Flask-SocketIO**, which integrates WebSockets directly into the application, simplifying the development of **chats, real-time notifications and interactive dashboards**.

Flask-SocketIO installation can be done with pip.

bash

```
pip install flask-socketio
```

Initial configuration requires creating an object SocketIO, which will manage WebSocket connections.

python

```
from flask import Flask
```

```python
from flask_socketio import SocketIO

app = Flask(__name__)
app.config["SECRET_KEY"] = "your_secret_key"
socketIO = SocketIO(app)

@app.route("/")
def index():
    return "WebSocket Server Running"

if __name__ == "__main__":
    socketio.run(app, debug=True)
```

This initializes a Flask server capable of managing WebSocket connections.

In order for clients to establish a connection, WebSocket events need to be defined.

python

```python
@socketio.on("message")
def handle_message(msg):
    print(f"Message received: {msg}")
    socketio.send(f"Echo: {msg}")
```

This event captures incoming messages and responds to them to the client, functioning as a **eco**.

Creating real-time chat with Flask-SocketIO

WebSockets are ideal for chat applications as they allow messages to be delivered instantly between connected users.

The structure of a chat requires three main components:

1. **Flask Server with WebSockets** to manage connections and message transmission.
2. **Frontend com WebSockets** to dynamically capture and display messages.
3. **Multiple user management** to allow simultaneous interactions.

The server can be configured to store logged in users and send messages between them.

python

```python
users = {}


@socketio.on("connect")
def handle_connect():
    print(f"User connected: {request.sid}")


@socketio.on("disconnect")
def handle_disconnect():
    print(f"User disconnected: {request.sid}")
    if request.sid in users:
        del users[request.sid]


@socketio.on("message")
def handle_message(data):
    user = users.get(request.sid, "Guest")
```

```
message = data.get("message")
socketio.emit("response", {"user": user, "message": message})
```

Each user is assigned a unique identifier (request.sid), allowing you to manage multiple connections simultaneously.

The frontend can be created using **JavaScript** to establish WebSocket connection and dynamically display messages.

html

```html
<!DOCTYPE html>
<html>
<head>
    <title>Real-time Chat</title>
</head>
<body>
    <ul id="messages"></ul>
    <input id="messageInput" type="text">
    <button onclick="sendMessage()">Send</button>

    <script src="https://cdnjs.cloudflare.com/ajax/libs/socket.io/4.0.1/socket.io.js"></script>
    <script>
        var socket = io();

        socket.on("response", function(data) {
            var that = document.createElement("that");
            li.textContent = data.user + ": " + data.message;
```

```
     document.getElementById("messages").appendChild(li
);

     });


     function sendMessage() {
     var message =
document.getElementById("messageInput").value;
     socket.send({"message": message});
     document.getElementById("messageInput").value = "";
     }
   </script>
</body>
</html>
```

This frontend allows messages to be typed and sent instantly to other users connected to WebSocket.

Integration with dynamic frontend

The integration of WebSockets with **dynamic interfaces** improves the interactivity of the application, allowing **automatic updates without reloading the page**.

To library **Flask-SocketIO** allows you to customize communication events to suit different types of applications, such as **system notifications, interactive dashboards and real-time data monitoring**.

Custom events can be set to send automatic notifications.

python

```
@socketio.on("notification")
```

```
def send_notification(data):
    socketio.emit("new_notification", {"title": data["title"],
"message": data["message"]})
```

On the frontend, notifications can be displayed dynamically.

html

```
<script>
    socket.on("new_notification", function(data) {
        alert(data.title + ": " + data.message);
    });


    function sendNotification() {
        socket.emit("notification", {"title": "New Alert", "message":
"Check your dashboard!"});
    }
</script>
```

This structure allows you to create alert systems, financial updates and monitoring dashboards that display new information in real time.

Common errors and how to resolve them

Error: WebSocket cannot connect to the server

Error message:

pgsql

WebSocket connection to 'ws://localhost:5000/socket.io/' failed

Probable cause: Flask server is not running with socketio.run(), or the WebSocket URL is incorrect.

Solution: Make sure you run the application correctly.

python

```
if __name__ == "__main__":
    socketio.run(app, debug=True)
```

Error: WebSocket event is not being received on the frontend

Error message:

vbnet

```
socket.emit is not a function
```

Probable cause: To library **Socket.IO** is not loaded correctly in the frontend.

Solution: Check that the script **Socket.IO** is imported correctly into HTML.

html

```
<script src="https://cdnjs.cloudflare.com/ajax/libs/socket.io/4.0.1/socket.io.js"></script>
```

Error: WebSocket server automatically disconnects

Error message:

nginx

```
WebSocket connection closed unexpectedly
```

Probable cause: The Flask server can be configured with **timeout curto** or WebSocket may be being terminated by firewall.

Solution: Adjust timeout time and check firewall settings.

python

```
socketio = SocketIO(app, ping_timeout=60)
```

The implementation of **WebSockets com Flask** allows you to create **interactive and responsive applications** without the need for continuous requests to the server.

PART 3: ADVANCED APPLICATIONS WITH FLASK

Flask application development is not just limited to the basic structure of routes, templates and standard database interactions. To create robust and scalable applications, it is essential to understand advanced practices that include **automated tests, integration with other technologies, deployment in optimized environments and advanced security**.

In this part of the book, the focus will be to deepen the knowledge previously acquired, presenting essential techniques for transforming a Flask application into a system **professional, scalable and secure**.

THE **Chapter 11** will address **automated tests**, an essential step to ensure the reliability of the application. You will be shown how to write **unit tests for routes and functions**, as well as integration tests for Flask APIs. The framework **pytest** will be used for test automation, allowing you to validate functionality before deploying the application.

THE **Chapter 12** will focus on **Flask application deployment**, addressing different strategies to put a system into production. will be explained **deploys on platforms like Heroku and Render**, as well as advanced settings with **Docker** for isolated environments. Deployment will also be covered in **VPS servers**, allowing greater control over resources.

THE **Chapter 13** will explore **integrations with other technologies**, allowing you to increase the efficiency and responsiveness of the application. will be addressed integrations with **Redis for caching, using Celery for asynchronous tasks** and **data storage in MongoDB** for applications that require NoSQL databases.

A **advanced security and authentication** will be the focus of **Chapter 14**, detailing how to implement **OAuth** for authentication via **Google, Facebook and GitHub**, in addition to authentication based on **tokens JWT**. Techniques will be demonstrated to ensure a secure system and **user authorization in Flask APIs**, preventing unauthorized access.

Finally, the **Chapter 15** will demonstrate how to integrate **artificial intelligence in Flask**, expanding the application possibilities. You will be shown how to create **a chatbot using Flask and OpenAI API**, in addition to applying **machine learning em APIs Flask**. Techniques for **image processing with OpenCV** will also be presented, allowing advanced manipulation of visual files within the application.

This part of the book will offer **essential skills for any Flask developer who wants to build modern, secure and scalable applications**. Mastering these practices will allow you to develop highly optimized systems, ready to be deployed in a production environment.

CHAPTER 11 – AUTOMATED TESTS IN FLASK

Writing unit tests for routes and functions

Flask application development requires that its functionalities be tested regularly to avoid failures. Test automation reduces the risk of errors by ensuring that new implementations or updates do not break essential parts of the system.

Unit tests validate specific parts of the application, such as **isolated functions, routes and database models**. Flask supports testing using the library **unittest**, which is already built into Python.

To start testing, the project structure must be organized correctly. Flask provides a **test client** to simulate HTTP requests without the need to run the real server.

The basic structure for testing can be organized as follows:

```bash
/my_flask_app
    /app
        __init__.py
        routes.py
    /tests
        test_routes.py
    run.py
```

THE **test client** can be created to simulate HTTP calls in application routes.

python

```python
import unittest
from app import app

class FlaskTestCase(unittest.TestCase):
    def setUp(self):
        app.config["TESTING"] = True
        self.client = app.test_client()

    def test_home_route(self):
        response = self.client.get("/")
        self.assertEqual(response.status_code, 200)
        self.assertIn(b"Welcome", response.data)

if __name__ == "__main__":
    unittest.main()
```

The method setUp() configures the test environment, ensuring that each test runs with a new Flask client. The method test_home_route() checks if the main route returns or status **200 OK** and contains the word **"Welcome"** in the answer.

To run the tests, simply run:

bash

```
python -m unittest discover tests
```

If the expected response does not correspond to the application's return, the error will be reported, allowing correction before deployment.

Integration tests for Flask APIs

Unit tests validate isolated functionalities, while integration tests check how different parts of the Flask application work together.

Flask APIs use **HTTP requests**, and integration tests simulate real calls to validate the full behavior of endpoints.

python

```python
class APITestCase(unittest.TestCase):
    def setUp(self):
        app.config["TESTING"] = True
        self.client = app.test_client()


    def test_get_users(self):
        response = self.client.get("/api/users")
        self.assertEqual(response.status_code, 200)
        self.assertEqual(response.content_type, "application/
json")


    def test_create_user(self):
        response = self.client.post("/api/users", json={"name":
"Alice", "email": "alice@example.com"})
        self.assertEqual(response.status_code, 201)
```

```
self.assertIn(b"User created", response.data)
```

This code tests a **endpoint GET** which returns users and a **endpoint POST** for creating users.

Integration tests help identify issues such as:

- **Incorrect API responses**
- **Lack of input validation**
- **Problems in communication between components**

To run the tests:

bash

```
python -m unittest tests/test_routes.py
```

If any test fails, the output will indicate exactly where the error occurred, making debugging easier.

Using pytest for automation

THE **pytest** is a more modern alternative to automated testing, offering a more concise syntax and better support for parameterization. Installation can be done with pip.

bash

```
pip install pytest
```

The structure of a test with **pytest** is simpler than with unittest.

python

```
import pytest
from app import app


@pytest.fixture
def client():
```

```
    app.config["TESTING"] = True
    return app.test_client()


def test_home(client):
    response = client.get("/")
    assert response.status_code == 200
    assert b"Welcome" in response.data
```

THE **pytest** deer **fixtures**, which simplify test environment setup. The fixture client() creates a reusable Flask client across all tests.

Tests are performed using:

bash

```
pytest
```

THE **pytest** displays detailed reports, clearly highlighting failures and successful tests.

The framework allows you to test various scenarios with **parameterization**.

python

```
@pytest.mark.parametrize("name, email, expected_status", [
    ("Alice", "alice@example.com", 201),
    ("", "invalid@example.com", 400),
    ("Bob", "", 400)
])
def test_create_user(client, name, email, expected_status):
```

```
    response = client.post("/api/users", json={"name": name,
"email": email})
    assert response.status_code == expected_status
```

This approach tests multiple cases with **different entries**, ensuring that validations are correct.

Common errors and how to resolve them

Error: Test fails due to lack of environment configuration

Error message:

makefile

RuntimeError: Working outside of application context.

Probable cause: The code attempted to access Flask resources without configuring the **application context**.

Solution: Utilize with app.app_context(): when accessing the database or settings.

python

```
with app.app_context():
    user_count = User.query.count()
```

Error: Test returns status 500 on an endpoint expected as 200

Error message:

yaml

AssertionError: 500 != 200

Probable cause: An internal error occurred on the Flask server.

Solution: Check Flask logs (app.run(debug=True)) to identify the source of the error.

Error: Test fails when comparing binary strings and text

Error message:

php

AssertionError: b'User created' not in 'User created successfully!'

Probable cause: Flask returns **binary data (b")** no response.data, while the test compares a normal string.

Solution: Decode response.data before comparison.

python

assert "User created" in response.data.decode("utf-8")

Test automation in Flask improves application reliability by ensuring functions and APIs operate as expected. The use of **unittest** and **pytest** allows you to test routes, validate APIs and avoid failures before deployment.

CHAPTER 12 – FLASK APPLICATION DEPLOYMENT

Creating a working Flask application is just the first step in making it available to users. THE deploy is the process of putting the application into production, allowing it to be accessed on the web in a secure and scalable way. There are several options for hosting a Flask application, each suited to different scenarios and needs.

Methods covered in this chapter include deploy no Heroku e Render, which are managed platforms that facilitate deployment without the need to configure servers, Docker, which allows you to package and run applications in containers, and deploy on VPS servers, offering full control over the infrastructure.

The choice of approach depends on factors such as ease of configuration, cost, scalability and control over the environment.

Configuration for deployment on Heroku and Render

Deploy no Heroku

THE **Heroku** is a cloud computing platform that allows you to host Flask applications without the need to manage servers. It supports Python natively and is one of the easiest options for quickly deploying applications.

Installing the Heroku CLI can be done via terminal:

bash

```
curl https://cli-assets.heroku.com/install.sh | sh
```

To start the deployment, you need a Git repository and a file requirements.txt listing application dependencies.

The creation of the requirements.txt can be done automatically:

bash

```
pip freeze > requirements.txt
```

Another essential file is the Procfile, which tells Heroku how to launch the application.

txt

```
web: gunicorn app:app
```

Gunicorn is a recommended WSGI server for running Flask in production. It can be installed with:

bash

```
pip install gunicorn
```

With the application ready, the deployment is carried out with the following commands:

bash

```
heroku login
heroku create my-flask-app
git add .
git commit -m "Deploy Flask app"
git push heroku main
```

After the process is complete, the application will be available at a URL automatically generated by Heroku.

Heroku offers a free environment, but applications that require scalability and higher performance can be moved to paid plans.

Deploy no Render

THE **Render** is an alternative to Heroku, offering free hosting for Flask applications and simplified support for continuous deployment.

The first step is to create an account on **Render** and connect a GitHub repository containing the application.

Required files include:

- **requirements.txt** with the dependencies
- **Procfile** to set the boot command
- **render.yaml** to configure the service

THE **render.yaml** can be structured like this:

yaml

```
services:
  - name: flask-app
    type: web
    runtime: python
    buildCommand: "pip install -r requirements.txt"
    startCommand: "gunicorn app:app"
```

After configuring the repository and configuring the settings in Render, simply deploy the application directly from the platform's web interface.

The advantage of **Render** is the simplicity of integration with GitHub and the possibility of carrying out **automatic deploys** with each new code update.

Environment configuration in Docker

THE **Docker** allows you to package your Flask application in a container, ensuring that it works consistently in any environment, regardless of operating system settings.

The creation of a **Dockerfile** defines the instructions for building the container.

dockerfile

```
FROM python:3.9


WORKDIR /app


COPY requirements.txt requirements.txt
RUN pip install -r requirements.txt


COPY . .


CMD ["gunicorn", "-b", "0.0.0.0:5000", "app:app"]
```

This Dockerfile performs the following steps:

- Uses a Python base image
- Sets the working directory
- Copy and install dependencies
- Copy the application code
- Start the application using **Gunicorn**

To build the Docker image:

bash

```
docker build -t flask-app
```

And to run the container locally:

bash

```
docker run -p 5000:5000 flask-app
```

Flask will be accessible at http://localhost:5000.

The next step is to host the container on a cloud service like **AWS, Google Cloud, Azure ou Docker Hub**.

THE **Docker Compose** allows you to run multiple containers simultaneously, useful for applications that include databases or external services.

The file docker-compose.yml can be used to define multiple services.

yaml

```
version: "3.8"
services:
  web:
    build: .
    ports:
      - "5000:5000"
    depends_on:
      - db
  db:
    image: postgres
```

```
environment:
  POSTGRES_USER: user
  POSTGRES_PASSWORD: password
```

To start all containers:

bash

```
docker-compose up
```

This allows you to run Flask alongside a PostgreSQL database without the need for manual installation.

Deploy on VPS servers

One **VPS (Virtual Private Server)** offers full control over the infrastructure, allowing you to configure the environment the way you want.

One of the most common methods for hosting Flask on a VPS is using **Nginx e Gunicorn**.

After connecting to the VPS via SSH:

bash

```
ssh user@server_ip
```

Install the required packages:

bash

```
sudo apt update && sudo apt install python3-pip python3-venv
nginx
```

Create a virtual environment and install dependencies:

bash

```
python3 -m venv venv
source venv/bin/activate
pip install flask gunicorn
```

Create a **systemd service** to run the application as an independent process.

bash

```
sudo nano /etc/systemd/system/flask_app.service
```

Add the following content:

ini

```
[Unit]
Description=Flask App
After=network.target


[Service]
User=free
WorkingDirectory=/home/ubuntu/my_flask_app
ExecStart=/home/ubuntu/my_flask_app/venv/bin/gunicorn -w 4 -b 0.0.0.0:8000 app:app


[Install]
WantedBy=multi-user.target
```

Reload the services and launch the application:

bash

```
sudo systemctl daemon-reload
```

```
sudo systemctl start flask_app
sudo systemctl enable flask_app
```

Configure the **Nginx** to act as a reverse proxy.

bash

```
sudo nano /etc/nginx/sites-available/flask_app
```

Add proxy configuration:

nginx

```
server {
    listen 80;
    server_name myflaskapp.com;

    location / {
        proxy_pass http://127.0.0.1:8000;
        proxy_set_header Host $host;
        proxy_set_header X-Real-IP $remote_addr;
    }
}
```

Activate the configuration and restart Nginx:

bash

```
sudo ln -s /etc/nginx/sites-available/flask_app /etc/nginx/sites-enabled
sudo systemctl restart nginx
```

This allows the application to be accessed via the web with a configured domain.

Deploying Flask applications can be carried out in several ways, from managed platforms like Heroku and Render, until custom environments with Docker and VPS. The choice of approach depends on the need for scalability, control over the environment, and ease of configuration.

CHAPTER 13 – FLASK AND INTEGRATION WITH OTHER TECHNOLOGIES

Flask's integration with other technologies is essential to increase the efficiency and scalability of applications. Many modern systems rely on caching to improve performance, asynchronous task execution to optimize processing of heavy operations, and flexible data storage using NoSQL databases.

Flask allows native integration with tools like Redis, which enables caching of responses and user sessions, Celery, which manages the execution of asynchronous tasks, and MongoDB, which offers flexibility to store structured and semi-structured data.

Proper use of these technologies significantly improves the performance, reliability and scalability of Flask applications.

Communication with Redis for caching

Redis is a database **in-memory** high-speed application used for caching, message queuing, and session storage. It reduces the load on the main database by storing answers to frequently accessed queries.

Redis installation can be done directly on the server with the command:

bash

```
sudo apt install redis
```

In the development environment, it can be used with Docker:

bash

```
docker run --name redis -p 6379:6379 -d redis
```

Integration with Flask can be done using the library **Flask-Caching**.

bash

```
pip install flask-caching
```

Configuring Redis as a cache system in Flask is performed through the object **Cache**.

python

```
from flask import Flask, jsonify
from flask_caching import Cache

app = Flask(__name__)
app.config["CACHE_TYPE"] = "RedisCache"
app.config["CACHE_REDIS_HOST"] = "localhost"
app.config["CACHE_REDIS_PORT"] = 6379

cache = Cache(app)

@app.route("/data")
@cache.cached(timeout=60)
def get_data():
```

```
    return jsonify({"message": "This response is cached for 60
seconds"})
```

The decorator @cache.cached(timeout=60) stores the route response for 60 seconds, reducing the need to recalculate the same information repeatedly.

Another useful feature of Redis is the storage of **user sessions**. To library **Flask-Session** allows this integration.

bash

```
pip install flask-session
```

The configuration sets Redis as the session backend.

python

```
from flask_session import Session


app.config["SESSION_TYPE"] = "redis"

app.config["SESSION_PERMANENT"] = False

app.config["SESSION_USE_SIGNER"] = True

app.config["SESSION_KEY_PREFIX"] = "flask_session:"

app.config["SESSION_REDIS"] =
redis.StrictRedis(host="localhost", port=6379,
decode_responses=True)


Session(app)
```

This ensures that user sessions are stored in Redis, avoiding traditional database overhead.

Integration with Celery for asynchronous tasks

Tasks that require time-consuming processing, such as **sending emails, generating reports and indexing data**, must be executed asynchronously so as not to block the server's response.

THE **Celery** is a tool that allows you to perform tasks in the background using **workers**. It can be integrated with Flask to process time-consuming operations without compromising application performance.

Installation can be done with:

bash

```
pip install celery
```

The initial configuration of Celery uses Redis as a broker to store task messages.

python

```
from celery import Celery


app.config["CELERY_BROKER_URL"] = "redis://localhost:6379/0"

app.config["CELERY_RESULT_BACKEND"] = "redis://localhost:6379/0"


celery = Celery(app.name,
broker=app.config["CELERY_BROKER_URL"])
celery.conf.update(app.config)
```

An asynchronous task can be defined using the decorator

@celery.task.

python

```
@celery.task
def send_email(recipient, subject, message):
    print(f"Sending email to {recipient} with subject {subject}")
    return f"Email sent to {recipient}"
```

The task execution can be done by calling delay().

python

```
send_email.delay("user@example.com", "Welcome!", "Thank you for signing up!")
```

To start the **workers** of Celery, you need to run:

bash

```
celery -A app.celery worker --loglevel=info
```

This allows tasks to run in parallel without blocking HTTP requests.

Using Flask with MongoDB

MongoDB is a database **NoSQL** which stores data in JSON format, allowing flexibility for applications that need to deal with information without a fixed schema. It is useful for Flask applications that need to store **logs, events and dynamic documents**.

MongoDB installation can be done with Docker.

bash

```
docker run --name mongo -p 27017:27017 -d mongo
```

To library **Flask-PyMongo** facilitates the connection between Flask and MongoDB.

bash

```
pip install flask-pymongo
```

The initial configuration defines the database URL.

python

```
from flask_pymongo import PyMongo


app.config["MONGO_URI"] = "mongodb://localhost:27017/mydatabase"
mongo = PyMongo(app)
```

Insertion of documents can be done using the collection users.

python

```
@app.route("/add_user", methods=["POST"])
def add_user():
    user = {"name": "Alice", "email": "alice@example.com"}
    mongo.db.users.insert_one(user)
    return "User added successfully!"
```

The user query returns all documents in the collection.

python

```
@app.route("/get_users", methods=["GET"])
```

```
def get_users():
    users = list(mongo.db.users.find({}, {"_id": 0}))
    return jsonify(users)
```

Unlike SQL databases, MongoDB allows you to store flexible documents, adapting well to applications that deal with **unstructured and high variability data.**

Common errors and solutions

Error: Connection refused when trying to access Redis

Error message:

vbnet

redis.exceptions.ConnectionError: Error 111 connecting to localhost:6379.

Probable cause: The Redis service is not running.

Solution: Check Redis status and start the service.

bash

```
sudo systemctl start redis
```

Error: Celery task is not running

Error message:

nginx

Received unregistered task

Probable cause: The Celery worker is not running or the application name is incorrect.

Solution: Make sure the workers are started correctly.

bash

```
celery -A app.celery worker --loglevel=info
```

Error: Failed to connect to MongoDB

Error message:

yaml

```
pymongo.errors.ServerSelectionTimeoutError: No servers
found
```

Probable cause: MongoDB is not running.

Solution: Start the database manually or using Docker.

bash

```
docker start mongo
```

Flask's integration with Redis, Celery and MongoDB allows applications to handle **cache, asynchronous tasks and NoSQL databases**, making them more scalable and efficient.

CHAPTER 14 – IMPLEMENTING OAUTH AND JWT AUTHENTICATION

Authentication is one of the most critical elements in developing Flask applications, ensuring that only authorized users have access to certain functionalities. Modern authentication methods go beyond the use of traditional login and password, allowing users to use trusted third parties, such as Google, Facebook and GitHub, to access their accounts.

Two widely used approaches are OAuth, which allows authentication via external providers, and JWT (JSON Web Tokens), which offers token-based authentication, often used in REST APIs to avoid the need for server-side sessions.

Creating authentication via Google, Facebook and GitHub

THE **OAuth 2.0** is an authentication protocol used by large platforms to allow secure login without exposing user credentials. Flask supports OAuth through the library **Authlib**, which simplifies integration with external providers.

Installation can be done with pip.

bash

```
pip install authlib
```

Initial configuration requires creating authentication credentials on each provider. The example below implements authentication via **Google**, but the structure is similar for Facebook and GitHub.

First, configure the OAuth client on Flask.

python

```python
from flask import Flask, redirect, url_for, session
from authlib.integrations.flask_client import OAuth


app = Flask(__name__)
app.secret_key = "your_secret_key"


oauth = OAuth(app)
google = oauth.register(
    name="google",
    client_id="YOUR_GOOGLE_CLIENT_ID",
    client_secret="YOUR_GOOGLE_CLIENT_SECRET",
    authorize_url="https://accounts.google.com/o/oauth2/auth",
    authorize_params=None,
    access_token_url="https://oauth2.googleapis.com/token",
    access_token_params=None,
    client_kwargs={"scope": "openid email profile"},
)
```

The function register() Configures the OAuth client for Google, providing the authentication URL, token obtaining endpoint, and required scopes.

Next, you need to create the login route.

python

```python
@app.route("/login/google")
def login():
    return google.authorize_redirect(url_for("authorize",
_external=True))
```

This route redirects the user to Google, where he authorizes the application to access his information. After authorization, Google redirects you back to the Flask application.

The callback route gets the user token and data.

python

```python
@app.route("/authorize")
def authorize():
    token = google.authorize_access_token()
    user_info = google.get("https://www.googleapis.com/
oauth2/v2/userinfo").json()
    session["user"] = user_info
    return f"User logged in: {user_info['email']}"
```

User data is stored in the Flask session, allowing the user to remain authenticated.

The same process can be applied to Facebook and GitHub by changing the provider URLs.

To **Facebook**, the register() it would be like this:

python

```python
facebook = oauth.register(
    name="facebook",
    client_id="YOUR_FACEBOOK_CLIENT_ID",
```

```
    client_secret="YOUR_FACEBOOK_CLIENT_SECRET",

    authorize_url="https://www.facebook.com/v10.0/dialog/
oauth",

    access_token_url="https://graph.facebook.com/v10.0/
oauth/access_token",

    client_kwargs={"scope": "email public_profile"},

)
```

To **GitHub**, the register() would have:

python

```
github = oauth.register(
    name="github",
    client_id="YOUR_GITHUB_CLIENT_ID",
    client_secret="YOUR_GITHUB_CLIENT_SECRET",
    authorize_url="https://github.com/login/oauth/authorize",
    access_token_url="https://github.com/login/oauth/
access_token",
    client_kwargs={"scope": "user:email"},
)
```

This allows the application to accept multiple authentication providers without storing passwords locally.

JWT token-based authentication

Unlike OAuth, which delegates authentication to external providers, OAuth **JWT (JSON Web Token)** is used to create **signed authentication tokens,** allowing authentication **without storing sessions on the server.**

Installation can be done with pip.

bash

```
pip install pyjwt flask-jwt-extended
```

The initial Flask-JWT-Extended configuration defines the secret key used to sign the tokens.

python

```
from flask import Flask, jsonify, request
from flask_jwt_extended import JWTManager,
create_access_token, jwt_required, get_jwt_identity


app = Flask(__name__)
app.config["JWT_SECRET_KEY"] = "your_secret_key"
jwt = JWTManager(app)
```

Create a route for authentication that generates a JWT token.

python

```
@app.route("/login", methods=["POST"])
def login():
    username = request.json.get("username")
    password = request.json.get("password")

    if username == "admin" and password == "password":
        access_token = create_access_token(identity=username)
        return jsonify(access_token=access_token)
```

```
return jsonify({"message": "Invalid credentials"}), 401
```

The endpoint receives user credentials and, if valid, returns a JWT token.

JWT tokens can be used to secure routes that require authentication.

python

```python
@app.route("/protected", methods=["GET"])
@jwt_required()
def protected():
    current_user = get_jwt_identity()
    return jsonify(message=f"Hello, {current_user}!")
```

When accessing this route without a valid token, the server returns **401 Unauthorized**.

To consume the protected API, the client must include the token in the request header.

bash

```bash
curl -H "Authorization: Bearer YOUR_ACCESS_TOKEN" http://localhost:5000/protected
```

JWT tokens are ideal for applications **SPA (Single Page Applications) e APIs REST**, eliminating the need to store sessions on the server.

Implementing authorization for Flask APIs

Authentication verifies the user's identity, while **authorization** determines what actions he can perform. The implementation of **roles and permissions** restricts access to certain endpoints.

The basic structure involves defining **roles** in the JWT token and validate these permissions before granting access.

When creating the token, you can add a user role.

python

```python
@app.route("/login", methods=["POST"])
def login():
    username = request.json.get("username")
    role = "admin" if username == "admin" else "user"


    access_token = create_access_token(identity={"username": username, "role": role})
    return jsonify(access_token=access_token)
```

In the protected route, authorization checks the user's role.

python

```python
from flask_jwt_extended import get_jwt


@app.route("/admin", methods=["GET"])
@jwt_required()
def admin():
    claims = get_jwt()
    if claims["sub"]["role"] != "admin":
        return jsonify({"message": "Access denied"}), 403


    return jsonify(message="Welcome, Admin!")
```

This prevents unauthorized users from accessing certain endpoints.

<h2 style="text-align:center">Common errors and solutions</h2>

Error: Invalid JWT Token

Error message:

nginx

Invalid token

Probable cause: The token has expired or been modified.

Solution: Regenerate a new token and ensure that the secret key is the same as the one used for signing.

Error: OAuth redirects to provider error

Error message:

nginx

Invalid client_id or redirect_uri

Probable cause: The application credentials are incorrect or the callback URL has not been configured in the provider panel.

Solution: Verify credentials and correctly register the **redirect_uri**.

Authentication and authorization are fundamental to any Flask application, allowing login via **OAuth (Google, Facebook, GitHub)** and authentication based on **JWT for REST APIs**.

CHAPTER 15 – FLASK APPLICATION WITH ARTIFICIAL INTELLIGENCE

Artificial intelligence has transformed the development of web applications, allowing systems to offer advanced functionalities, such as chatbots, predictive analytics, computer vision and natural language processing. Flask, combined with specialized libraries, makes it possible to integrate AI models directly into web applications and APIs.

This chapter will cover three practical applications of AI in Flask: creating chatbots using the OpenAI API, the incorporation of machine learning em APIs Flask and the processing of images with OpenCV.

Creating a chatbot with Flask and OpenAI API

Chatbots are one of the most popular applications of AI, being used for customer support, task automation and interactive assistance. OpenAI provides a powerful API to generate intelligent responses based on natural language.

To get started, you need to install the library **openai**.

bash

```
pip install openai flask
```

The initial configuration of the chatbot requires defining the API key.

python

```python
import openai
from flask import Flask, request, jsonify


app = Flask(__name__)
openai.api_key = "YOUR_OPENAI_API_KEY"


@app.route("/chatbot", methods=["POST"])
def chatbot():
    user_input = request.json.get("message")
    response = openai.ChatCompletion.create(
        model="gpt-4",
        messages=[{"role": "user", "content": user_input}]
    )
    return jsonify({"response": response["choices"][0]["message"]["content"]})


if __name__ == "__main__":
    app.run(debug=True)
```

The endpoint receives a message from the user and returns a response generated by the **GPT-4**. The model can be adjusted to customize the chatbot's behavior.

The frontend can be integrated using JavaScript.

html

```html
<script>
    async function sendMessage() {
```

```
    let message =
document.getElementById("userInput").value;

    let response = await fetch("/chatbot", {

        method: "POST",

        headers: {"Content-Type": "application/json"},

        body: JSON.stringify({"message": message})

    });

    let data = await response.json();

    document.getElementById("response").innerText =
data.response;

    }

</script>

<input id="userInput" type="text">

<button onclick="sendMessage()">Send</button>

<p id="response"></p>
```

This integration allows you to create intuitive conversational interfaces, useful for **support, recommendations and virtual assistants**.

Aplicando Machine Learning em APIs Flask

Incorporating machine learning into Flask APIs allows you to predict results and classify data automatically. Learning models can be trained using libraries such as **scikit-learn**, **TensorFlow** or **PyTorch** and integrated into web applications.

Installing the libraries can be done with:

bash

pip install scikit-learn pandas flask

As an example, a model of **feelings classification** will be loaded into a Flask API for text analysis.

python

```python
import pickle
import pandas as pd
from flask import Flask, request, jsonify
from sklearn.feature_extraction.text import TfidfVectorizer


app = Flask(__name__)

with open("sentiment_model.pkl", "rb") as file:
    model, vectorizer = pickle.load(file)


@app.route("/predict", methods=["POST"])
def predict():
    text = request.json.get("text")
    vectorized_text = vectorizer.transform([text])
    prediction = model.predict(vectorized_text)[0]
    return jsonify({"sentiment": "positive" if prediction == 1 else "negative"})


if __name__ == "__main__":
    app.run(debug=True)
```

This code loads a pre-trained model of **sentiment analysis**, receives a text via API and returns whether the content has a **positive or negative rating**.

Model training can be done with an evaluation dataset.

python

```python
from sklearn.feature_extraction.text import TfidfVectorizer
from sklearn.naive_bayes import MultinomialNB
from sklearn.pipeline import make_pipeline
import pickle


texts = ["I love this!", "This is terrible", "Amazing product", "Worst experience"]
labels = [1, 0, 1, 0]


vectorizer = TfidfVectorizer()
model = make_pipeline(vectorizer, MultinomialNB())
model.fit(texts, labels)


with open("sentiment_model.pkl", "wb") as file:
    pickle.dump((model, vectorizer), file)
```

After training, the API can be used to analyze texts sent by users, allowing the construction of **automatic feedback tools, content moderation and smart support**.

Flask and image processing with OpenCV

Computer vision enables the manipulation and analysis

of images for facial recognition, object detection and segmentation. THE **OpenCV** is one of the main libraries for image processing and can be integrated with Flask to create APIs that process files uploaded by users.

Installation can be done with:

bash

```
pip install opencv-python-headless flask
```

The API can be structured to accept image uploads and convert color files to grayscale.

python

```
import cv2
import numpy as np
from flask import Flask, request, jsonify
from werkzeug.utils import secure_filename


app = Flask(__name__)
app.config["UPLOAD_FOLDER"] = "./uploads"


@app.route("/upload", methods=["POST"])
def upload_image():
    if "file" not in request.files:
        return jsonify({"error": "No file uploaded"}), 400


    file = request.files["file"]
    filename = secure_filename(file.filename)
```

```
filepath = f"{app.config['UPLOAD_FOLDER']}/{filename}"
file.save(filepath)


image = cv2.imread(filepath, cv2.IMREAD_GRAYSCALE)
output_path = f"{app.config['UPLOAD_FOLDER']}/
gray_{filename}"
cv2.imwrite(output_path, image)


return jsonify({"message": "Image processed", "path":
output_path})


if __name__ == "__main__":
app.run(debug=True)
```

This API allows users to upload images, which are converted to grayscale and stored on the server.

Conversion can be tested by uploading an image with cURL.

bash

```
curl -X POST -F "file=@image.jpg" http://localhost:5000/upload
```

The response will return the path of the processed file.

This approach can be expanded to include **facial detection, image segmentation and text reading (OCR)**, allowing you to develop advanced visual analysis applications.

Common errors and solutions

Error: OpenAI API does not respond correctly

Probable cause: The API key is incorrect or account limits have been reached.

Solution: Verify credentials and, if necessary, request a new token from OpenAI.

Error: Machine learning model cannot find training file

Probable cause: The file .street was not loaded correctly.

Solution: Ensure the file path is correct and the template is saved and loaded correctly.

Error: Failed to process image in OpenCV

Probable cause: The uploaded file is not a valid image.

Solution: Check the file format before processing it.

python

```
if not file.filename.lower().endswith(('.png', '.jpg', '.jpeg')):
    return jsonify({"error": "Invalid file format"}), 400
```

Integrating artificial intelligence with Flask allows you to create innovative applications that answer questions, analyze feelings and process images.

PART 4: BUILDING A COMPLETE PROJECT

After exploring the fundamentals of Flask, its application in building APIs, advanced techniques and strategic integrations, it's time to consolidate all the learning into one **complete and functional project**. The aim of this part of the book is **guide the reader in creating a real Flask application, structured from scratch, covering all necessary steps for a robust, secure and scalable system.**

The journey begins at **Chapter 16**, where the **definition of the final project**, addressing criteria for choosing a viable, challenging and applicable idea in the real world. Furthermore, it will be shown how **plan the application architecture, separating the backend, frontend and auxiliary services.**

THE **Chapter 17** deepens the construction of the **application backend**, implementing the **database, creating models and developing business logic**. This step focuses on efficiently structuring data, ensuring consistency and integrity.

No **Chapter 18**, attention turns to the construction of **APIs and backend services**, addressing **the creation of RESTful endpoints, secure authentication and user authorization**. Correct API design allows the application to be modular, reusable, and easy to integrate with other platforms.

The system interface will be worked on in **Chapter 19**, which teaches **create a dynamic frontend with Flask and Bootstrap**. Techniques for using **templates Jinja2**, ensuring **fluid navigation, responsive styling and good user experience**.

THE **Chapter 20** focuses on **application optimization and**

performance, exploring **caching, query optimization and efficient use of assets** to ensure **fast responses and better scalability**.

To maintain system stability, the **Chapter 21** introduce **error logging and monitoring strategies**. Setting up structured logs and integrating with tools like **Sentry** ensure that faults are quickly detected and resolved.

Safety will be the focus of **Chapter 22**, covering **protection against common attacks, permissions management and advanced authentication**. Applications that deal with sensitive data need to follow good security practices to avoid vulnerabilities.

THE **Chapter 23** deals with **scalability and integration with cloud services**, detailing **how to prepare a Flask application for heavy traffic and integration with AWS and Google Cloud**.

No **Chapter 24**, the application will be ready to be **published and maintained**, addressing **versioning, code maintenance and continuous deployment strategies** to ensure secure and efficient updates.

Finally, the **Chapter 25** it presents **the future trends of Flask and web development**, discussing **upcoming innovations, emerging technologies and pathways for continuous learning**, helping developers to evolve in their careers and improve their skills.

At the end of this part, the reader will have built a complete Flask application, going through **planning, backend, frontend, security, optimization, scalability and production publishing**. This practical experience will provide a solid foundation to develop new projects, explore new technologies and advance professionally in web development.

CHAPTER 16 – DEFINITION OF THE FINAL PROJECT

Creating a complete application requires planning and organization to ensure efficient, scalable and secure development. The objective of this chapter is to define a realistic and challenging project, which allows you to consolidate Flask learning throughout the book. Correctly structuring the application from the beginning avoids rework and technical problems as development progresses.

The choice of project must consider factors such as complexity suitable for the developer level, applicability in the real world, need for integration with databases and APIs and the possibility of future expansion. A well-planned project allows the implementation of essential features such as user authentication, data manipulation and dynamic interactions with the frontend.

The application will be designed to function as a Task Management System, allowing users to create, edit, delete and organize their tasks into categories. This type of system involves essential Flask concepts, including routes, database models, authentication, dynamic templates and performance optimization.

The project structure will be modular, separating responsibilities into different layers. This organization facilitates maintenance, scalability and integration with new features in the future.

Choosing a realistic and challenging project

Defining the project scope is essential to avoid complications during development. Very simple applications may not exploit all of Flask's functionality, while overly complex projects may become difficult to implement within the time available.

THE **Task Management System** meets these guidelines by including the following aspects:

- **Relational database** to store tasks, users and categories
- **Authentication and authorization** to ensure each user only manages their own tasks
- **APIs RESTful** to interact with the system in an efficient and modular way
- **Dynamic frontend** using Jinja2 and Bootstrap templates to improve user experience
- **Caching implementation and optimization** to improve performance
- **Integration with cloud services** to store data and allow scalability

This project can be expanded in the future to include integration with email notifications, a task sharing system between users and support for multiple devices.

The system structure can be represented as follows:

arduino

```
/task_manager
    /app
        __init__.py
        models.py
        routes.py
        auth.py
        static/
        templates/
    /migrations
```

config.py

run.py

requirements.txt

Each file and directory has a specific function in the operation of the application.

- models.py: defines the database tables and their relationships
- routes.py: contains the application routes, responsible for communication between frontend and backend
- auth.py: manages user authentication and authorization
- templates/: stores the HTML files used in the frontend
- static/: contains CSS files, JavaScript and images
- migrations/: records changes to the database
- config.py: Configures Flask settings such as security keys and database connection

This modular structure allows each part of the application to be developed independently, facilitating maintenance and expansion of the project.

Structuring the application from scratch

Building the application begins by creating the development environment. The use of a **virtual environment** ensures that all application dependencies are installed correctly and avoids conflicts with other projects in the system.

The virtual environment can be created and activated with the following commands:

bash

```
python3 -m venv venv

source venv/bin/activate  # No Windows: venv\Scripts\activate

pip install flask flask-sqlalchemy flask-login flask-migrate
```

Flask will be used to manage application routes, which **SQLAlchemy** to deal with the database, the **Flask-Login** for authentication and the **Flask-Migrate** for migration control.

The file config.py will be created to store global settings.

python

import them

class Config:

    SECRET_KEY = os.getenv("SECRET_KEY", "supersecretkey")

    SQLALCHEMY_DATABASE_URI = "sqlite:///tasks.db"

    SQLALCHEMY_TRACK_MODIFICATIONS = False

THE **SECRET_KEY** protects the application against request forgery attacks, while SQLALCHEMY_DATABASE_URI defines the connection to an SQLite database.

The database will be initialized to the file models.py, where the main tables will be defined.

python

from flask_sqlalchemy import SQLAlchemy

from flask_login import UserMixin

db = SQLAlchemy()

class User(db.Model, UserMixin):

    id = db.Column(db.Integer, primary_key=True)

```
    username = db.Column(db.String(50), unique=True,
nullable=False)
    password = db.Column(db.String(100), nullable=False)


class Task(db.Model):
    id = db.Column(db.Integer, primary_key=True)
    title = db.Column(db.String(100), nullable=False)
    description = db.Column(db.Text, nullable=True)
    completed = db.Column(db.Boolean, default=False)
    user_id = db.Column(db.Integer, db.ForeignKey("user.id"),
nullable=False)
```

The model **User** represents the users registered in the system, while the model **Task** stores the tasks associated with each user.

With the database structure defined, the tables will be created using **Flask-Migrate**.

bash
```
flask db init
flask db migrate -m "Initial migration"
flask db upgrade
```

The next step involves implementing the **application routes**, allowing users to interact with the system. The file routes.py will contain the main functionalities.

python
```
from flask import Flask, render_template, redirect, url_for,
request
```

```python
from flask_sqlalchemy import SQLAlchemy
from flask_login import LoginManager, UserMixin, login_user,
login_required, logout_user


app = Flask(__name__)
app.config.from_object("config.Config")


db.init_app(app)
login_manager = LoginManager(app)


@login_manager.user_loader
def load_user(user_id):
    return User.query.get(int(user_id))


@app.route("/")
def home():
    return render_template("index.html")


@app.route("/login", methods=["GET", "POST"])
def login():
    if request.method == "POST":
        username = request.form["username"]
        user = User.query.filter_by(username=username).first()
        if user:
            login_user(user)
```

```python
        return redirect(url_for("dashboard"))
    return render_template("login.html")


@app.route("/dashboard")
@login_required
def dashboard():
    return render_template("dashboard.html")


@app.route("/logout")
def logout():
    logout_user()
    return redirect(url_for("home"))
```

This code initializes the Flask application, configures authentication, and defines main routes.

The application frontend will be developed using **Bootstrap e Jinja2**, allowing you to create a dynamic and responsive interface. The file templates/index.html will serve as the home page.

html

```html
<!DOCTYPE html>
<html lang="yes">
<head>
    <title>Task Manager</title>
    <link rel="stylesheet" href="https://cdn.jsdelivr.net/npm/bootstrap@5.3.0/dist/css/bootstrap.min.css">
```

```
</head>
<body>
   <div class="container">
      <h1 class="mt-5">Welcome to Task Manager</h1>
      <a href="{{ url_for('login') }}" class="btn btn-primary
mt-3">Login</a>
   </div>
</body>
</html>
```

The initial project structure is complete, allowing users to log in and access the restricted area.

The project will evolve to include task management, RESTful APIs, advanced security and performance optimizations.

CHAPTER 17 – CREATING THE APPLICATION BACKEND

The backend of a Flask application is responsible for managing data, business logic and interaction with the database. It defines models, relationships between tables, authentication and validations, ensuring that the application works correctly and securely.

Building the backend begins with defining the database structure, using Flask-SQLAlchemy for efficient data manipulation. Furthermore, business logic will be implemented, organizing the functions responsible for creating, editing, deleting and retrieving information.

This chapter details the implementation of the database, creation of models, configuration of tables and organization of business logic, preparing the application to work in a modular and scalable way.

Implementing the database

The database will store **information about users, tasks and categories**, allowing data to be retrieved and manipulated efficiently.

To library **Flask-SQLAlchemy** has already been installed in the virtual environment and will be used to create the bank's models. The first step is to initialize the database in the file models.py.

python

```
from flask_sqlalchemy import SQLAlchemy
```

```python
from flask_login import UserMixin
```

```python
db = SQLAlchemy()
```

The connection to the bank will be defined in the file config.py, where the application will be configured to use **SQLite**.

python

```python
import them
```

```python
class Config:
    SECRET_KEY = os.getenv("SECRET_KEY", "supersecretkey")
    SQLALCHEMY_DATABASE_URI = "sqlite:///tasks.db"
    SQLALCHEMY_TRACK_MODIFICATIONS = False
```

This configuration ensures that the application has a **secret key for security** and use a local database to store the information.

With the framework configured, templates can be defined.

Creating models and business logic

The database will contain **three main tables**:

- **User**: Stores users' login and authentication information
- **Task**: records tasks created, completion status and relationships with users
- **Category**: Allows you to organize tasks into custom categories

The models will be defined in the models.py.

python

```python
class User(db.Model, UserMixin):
    id = db.Column(db.Integer, primary_key=True)
    username = db.Column(db.String(50), unique=True,
nullable=False)
    password = db.Column(db.String(100), nullable=False)
    tasks = db.relationship("Task", backref="user", lazy=True)


class Category(db.Model):
    id = db.Column(db.Integer, primary_key=True)
    name = db.Column(db.String(50), unique=True,
nullable=False)
    tasks = db.relationship("Task", backref="category",
lazy=True)


class Task(db.Model):
    id = db.Column(db.Integer, primary_key=True)
    title = db.Column(db.String(100), nullable=False)
    description = db.Column(db.Text, nullable=True)
    completed = db.Column(db.Boolean, default=False)
    user_id = db.Column(db.Integer, db.ForeignKey("user.id"),
nullable=False)
    category_id = db.Column(db.Integer,
db.ForeignKey("category.id"), nullable=True)
```

Each table has its well-defined fields:

- **User**: includes username and password, in addition to the relationship with the tasks

- **Category**: stores name, allowing you to group tasks
- **Task**: contains title, description, completed, user_id (linking the task to the user) and category_id (associating a category)

The creation of the database will be done using **Flask-Migrate**, which allows you to apply changes without losing information already recorded.

In the terminal, the following commands create and apply the migration:

bash

```
flask db init

flask db migrate -m "Initial migration"

flask db upgrade
```

This generates the structure of the tables in the database.

With the models defined, the business logic will be implemented in **functions to create, update, delete and search tasks and users.**

Inserting a new user into the database can be done in the **record.**

python

```
from flask_bcrypt import Bcrypt


bcrypt = Bcrypt()


def register_user(username, password):
    hashed_password =
bcrypt.generate_password_hash(password).decode("utf-8")
    new_user = User(username=username,
```

```
password=hashed_password)
    db.session.add(new_user)
    db.session.commit()
    return new_user
```

The above function **encrypt the password** before storing it in the database.

To retrieve a user during login, the authentication function will check the credentials.

python

```
def authenticate_user(username, password):
    user = User.query.filter_by(username=username).first()
    if user and bcrypt.check_password_hash(user.password, password):
        return user
    return None
```

This allows you to validate users before granting access to the application.

The creation of a new task will be carried out with the following function:

python

```
def create_task(title, description, user_id, category_id=None):
    task = Task(title=title, description=description, user_id=user_id, category_id=category_id)
    db.session.add(task)
    db.session.commit()
```

```
    return task
```

The function adds a new task linked to the user and, optionally, a category.

To retrieve a user's tasks, the following role will be created:

python

```python
def get_tasks_by_user(user_id):
    return Task.query.filter_by(user_id=user_id).all()
```

This query returns all tasks registered by a specific user.

Updating the status of a task can be done like this:

python

```python
def update_task_status(task_id, completed):
    task = Task.query.get(task_id)
    if task:
        task.completed = completed
        db.session.commit()
        return task
    return None
```

Removing a task from the bank will be done through:

python

```python
def delete_task(task_id):
    task = Task.query.get(task_id)
    if task:
```

```
db.session.delete(task)

db.session.commit()
```

These functions ensure that **create, read, update, and delete (CRUD) operations** are carried out efficiently in the database.

Organizing the backend structure

To maintain code modularity, the structure will be organized by separating **models, business logic and routes**.

bash

```
/task_manager

  /app

    __init__.py

    models.py

    database.py

    services.py

    routes.py
```

- **models.py**: defines the structure of the database tables
- **database.py**: contains the database and initialization configuration
- **services.py**: stores business logic (CRUD)
- **routes.py**: manages API requests

The file database.py initializes the database.

python

```
from flask import Flask

from flask_sqlalchemy import SQLAlchemy


db = SQLAlchemy()
```

```python
def init_db(app):
    db.init_app(app)
    with app.app_context():
        db.create_all()
```

The file __init__.py configures Flask and imports the database.
python

```python
from flask import Flask
from .database import init_db
from .routes import app_routes


def create_app():
    app = Flask(__name__)
    app.config.from_object("config.Config")

    init_db(app)
    app.register_blueprint(app_routes)

    return app
```

With this modular organization, the application becomes **more maintainable and scalable**.

The backend is now prepared to manage users and tasks

efficiently, allowing the next chapter to move into **creation of RESTful APIs**, which will enable communication with the frontend and external services.

CHAPTER 18 – BUILDING APIS AND BACKEND SERVICES

The backend of a Flask application can be structured to provide RESTful APIs, enabling efficient communication between the frontend, external services, and other systems. Defining clear and well-organized endpoints makes the API easy to consume, ensuring that each functionality has a well-documented interface.

In addition to defining endpoints, implementing authentication and authorization ensures that only authorized users can access certain routes. Flask offers robust support for JWT, OAuth, and session-based authentication.

Correctly structuring the API allows the application to function in a modular, scalable and secure manner, facilitating future expansions and integrations.

Defining endpoints and RESTful structure

The architecture **REST (Representational State Transfer)** defines a set of best practices for creating organized and scalable APIs. A RESTful API follows principles such as:

- **Using HTTP methods**: GET to fetch data, POST for creation, PUT for updating and DELETE for removal
- **Intuitive URLs**: /tasks to list tasks, /tasks/1 to access a specific task
- **Return of standardized responses**: Using JSON as a communication format
- **Stateless**: Each request must contain all the information necessary to be processed

A API do **Task Manager** will be structured with the following endpoints:

Method	Endpoint	Description
POST	/register	Create a new user
POST	/login	Authenticates a user
GET	/tasks	List all user tasks
POST	/tasks	Create a new task
GET	/tasks/<id>	Returns a specific task
PUT	/tasks/<id>	Update a task
DELETE	/tasks/<id>	Remove a task

The implementation of these routes begins with the creation of the file routes.py.

python

```python
from flask import Blueprint, request, jsonify
from flask_jwt_extended import jwt_required, get_jwt_identity
from .models import db, Task, User
from flask_jwt_extended import create_access_token


app_routes = Blueprint("app_routes", __name__)


@app_routes.route("/register", methods=["POST"])
def register():
```

```python
    data = request.json
    if not data.get("username") or not data.get("password"):
        return jsonify({"error": "Username and password
required"}), 400


    if User.query.filter_by(username=data["username"]).first():
        return jsonify({"error": "User already exists"}), 409


    new_user = User(username=data["username"],
password=data["password"])
    db.session.add(new_user)
    db.session.commit()


    return jsonify({"message": "User registered successfully"}),
201


@app_routes.route("/login", methods=["POST"])
def login():
    data = request.json
    user =
User.query.filter_by(username=data["username"]).first()


    if user and user.password == data["password"]:
        access_token = create_access_token(identity=user.id)
        return jsonify({"access_token": access_token})
```

```python
    return jsonify({"error": "Invalid credentials"}), 401
```

Authentication uses **JWT (JSON Web Token)** to generate a token for the user who logs in. This token will be used to access the API's protected routes.

Task creation occurs through the endpoint /tasks, ensuring that each task is associated with the authenticated user.

python

```python
@app_routes.route("/tasks", methods=["POST"])
@jwt_required()
def create_task():
    data = request.json
    user_id = get_jwt_identity()

    if not data.get("title"):
        return jsonify({"error": "Task title required"}), 400

    task = Task(title=data["title"],
description=data.get("description"), user_id=user_id)
    db.session.add(task)
    db.session.commit()

    return jsonify({"message": "Task created successfully",
"task_id": task.id}), 201
```

Tasks can be consulted with the route **GET /tasks**, returning all tasks for the authenticated user.

python

```python
@app_routes.route("/tasks", methods=["GET"])
@jwt_required()
def get_tasks():
    user_id = get_jwt_identity()
    tasks = Task.query.filter_by(user_id=user_id).all()


    return jsonify([{"id": t.id, "title": t.title, "description": t.description, "completed": t.completed} for t in tasks])
```

Updating tasks allows you to change the title, description, or status.

python

```python
@app_routes.route("/tasks/<int:task_id>", methods=["PUT"])
@jwt_required()
def update_task(task_id):
    data = request.json
    user_id = get_jwt_identity()
    task = Task.query.filter_by(id=task_id, user_id=user_id).first()


    if not task:
        return jsonify({"error": "Task not found"}), 404
```

```python
task.title = data.get("title", task.title)
task.description = data.get("description", task.description)
task.completed = data.get("completed", task.completed)
db.session.commit()


return jsonify({"message": "Task updated successfully"})
```

Deleting tasks requires authentication and validation from the task owner.

python

```python
@app_routes.route("/tasks/<int:task_id>",
methods=["DELETE"])

@jwt_required()

def delete_task(task_id):
    user_id = get_jwt_identity()

    task = Task.query.filter_by(id=task_id,
user_id=user_id).first()


    if not task:
        return jsonify({"error": "Task not found"}), 404


    db.session.delete(task)
    db.session.commit()
```

```
return jsonify({"message": "Task deleted successfully"})
```

Implementing authentication and authorization

Authentication has already been structured using **JWT**, ensuring that each user has a token to access protected routes.

Authorization defines **who can access and modify data**, ensuring that one user cannot change tasks from another.

Protections are implemented using @jwt_required() and checks within each endpoint.

If a user tries to access a task that does not belong to him, the API returns **403 Forbidden**.

python

```python
if task.user_id != user_id:
    return jsonify({"error": "Unauthorized"}), 403
```

To avoid **invalid or expired tokens**, the JWT configuration can include an expiration time.

python

```python
app.config["JWT_ACCESS_TOKEN_EXPIRES"] = timedelta(hours=1)
```

This ensures that the tokens have a limited validity, reducing the risk of improper access.

The implementation of **user roles** can be done by adding a column role on the table **User**.

python

```
class User(db.Model):
    id = db.Column(db.Integer, primary_key=True)
    username = db.Column(db.String(50), unique=True,
nullable=False)
    password = db.Column(db.String(100), nullable=False)
    role = db.Column(db.String(20), default="user")
```

To validate permissions on administrative routes, simply include a validation decorator.

python

```
def admin_required(fn):
    @wraps(fn)
    def wrapper(*args, **kwargs):
        user_id = get_jwt_identity()
        user = User.query.get(user_id)
        if user.role != "admin":
            return jsonify({"error": "Admin access required"}), 403
        return fn(*args, **kwargs)
    return wrapper


@app_routes.route("/admin/dashboard")
@jwt_required()
@admin_required
def admin_dashboard():
    return jsonify({"message": "Welcome, admin!"})
```

This implementation ensures that only administrators can access certain routes.

The API is now structured with well-defined endpoints, JWT authentication, per-user authorization and reinforced security.

CHAPTER 19 – CREATING THE WEB INTERFACE WITH FLASK AND BOOTSTRAP

The web interface is responsible for the user experience when interacting with the application. In Flask, this is done using Jinja2 templates, which allow you to create dynamic and reusable pages. Additionally, Bootstrap will be used to style the application, ensuring a responsive and modern layout.

Building the frontend will be divided into two parts: creating Jinja2 templates for rendering dynamic pages and integrating with Bootstrap for a professional design.

Applying Jinja2 templates for dynamic interfaces

Jinja2 is a templating system that allows you to embed logic within HTML. It makes it possible to insert variables, perform loops and conditionals, reuse components and structure layouts efficiently.

The structure of the templates will be organized as follows:

bash

```
/task_manager
    /app
        /templates
            base.html
            index.html
            login.html
```

dashboard.html

tasks.html

The file base.html will serve as a **template base**, avoiding code repetition and ensuring that all pages have a uniform layout.

html

```
<!DOCTYPE html>
<html lang="yes">
<head>
    <meta charset="UTF-8">
    <meta name="viewport" content="width=device-width, initial-scale=1.0">
    <title>{% block title %}Task Manager{% endblock %}</title>
    <link rel="stylesheet" href="https://cdn.jsdelivr.net/npm/bootstrap@5.3.0/dist/css/bootstrap.min.css">
</head>
<body>
    <nav class="navbar navbar-expand-lg navbar-dark bg-dark">
        <div class="container">
            <a class="navbar-brand" href="{{ url_for('home') }}">Task Manager</a>
            <div class="collapse navbar-collapse">
                <ul class="navbar-nav ms-auto">
                    {% if current_user.is_authenticated %}
                        <li class="nav-item">
                            <a class="nav-link" href="{{ url_for('dashboard') }}">Dashboard</a>
```

```
            </li>
            <li class="nav-item">
                <a class="nav-link"
href="{{ url_for('logout') }}">Logout</a>
            </li>
        {% else %}
            <li class="nav-item">
                <a class="nav-link"
href="{{ url_for('login') }}">Login</a>
            </li>
        {% endif %}
        </ul>
      </div>
    </div>
  </none>
  <div class="container mt-4">
    {% block content %}{% endblock %}
  </div>
</body>
</html>
```

This file contains the main structure of the application, including **navigation bar, dynamic links and area reserved for page content.**

The home page (index.html) will be rendered in Flask to display an introduction to the application.

html

```
{% extends "base.html" %}

{% block title %}Welcome{% endblock %}

{% block content %}
<div class="text-center">
    <h1>Welcome to Task Manager</h1>
    <p class="lead">Organize your tasks efficiently.</p>
    <a href="{{ url_for('login') }}" class="btn btn-primary">Login</a>
</div>
{% endblock %}
```

This approach avoids code repetition and ensures that any layout changes are applied to all pages.

Login will be structured on the page login.html.

html

```
{% extends "base.html" %}

{% block title %}Login{% endblock %}

{% block content %}
<div class="row justify-content-center">
    <div class="col-md-4">
        <h2 class="text-center">Login</h2>
```

```html
<form method="POST">
    <div class="mb-3">
        <label for="username" class="form-label">Username</label>
        <input type="text" class="form-control" id="username" name="username" required>
    </div>
    <div class="mb-3">
        <label for="password" class="form-label">Password</label>
        <input type="password" class="form-control" id="password" name="password" required>
    </div>
    <button type="submit" class="btn btn-primary w-100">Login</button>
</form>
</div>
</div>
{% endblock %}
```

In Flask, the login route will render this page and process the credentials.

python

```python
from flask import render_template, request, redirect, url_for
from flask_login import login_user, current_user
from .models import User
```

```
@app.route("/login", methods=["GET", "POST"])
def login():
    if request.method == "POST":
        username = request.form["username"]
        password = request.form["password"]
        user = User.query.filter_by(username=username).first()

        if user and user.password == password:
            login_user(user)
            return redirect(url_for("dashboard"))

    return render_template("login.html")
```

Styling the application with Bootstrap

THE **Bootstrap** allows you to style the interface without having to create CSS from scratch. It provides **pre-defined components for responsive buttons, forms, tables and panels**.

The page of **dashboard** will display the user's tasks and allow the creation of new tasks.

html

```
{% extends "base.html" %}

{% block title %}Dashboard{% endblock %}
```

```
{% block content %}
<h2>Task Dashboard</h2>

<table class="table table-striped">
    <thead>
        <tr>
            <th>Title</th>
            <th>Description</th>
            <th>Status</th>
            <th>Actions</th>
        </tr>
    </thead>
    <tbody>
        {% for task in tasks %}
        <tr>
            <td>{{ task.title }}</td>
            <td>{{ task.description }}</td>
            <td>
                {% if task.completed %}
                    <span class="badge bg-success">Completed</span>
                {% else %}
                    <span class="badge bg-warning">Pending</span>
                {% endif %}
```

```
        </td>
        <td>
            <a href="{{ url_for('edit_task', task_id=task.id) }}"
class="btn btn-sm btn-warning">Edit</a>
            <a href="{{ url_for('delete_task', task_id=task.id) }}"
class="btn btn-sm btn-danger">Delete</a>
        </td>
    </tr>
    {% endfor %}
  </tbody>
</table>


<h3>Add New Task</h3>
<form method="POST">
    <div class="mb-3">
        <label for="title" class="form-label">Title</label>
        <input type="text" class="form-control" id="title"
name="title" required>
    </div>
    <div class="mb-3">
        <label for="description" class="form-label">Description</
label>
        <textarea class="form-control" id="description"
name="description"></textarea>
    </div>
    <button type="submit" class="btn btn-success">Add Task</
button>
```

```
</form>
{% endblock %}
```

No Flask, a rota do **dashboard** will manage the listing and creation of tasks.

python

```python
from flask import render_template, request, redirect, url_for
from flask_login import login_required, current_user
from .models import db, Task


@app.route("/dashboard", methods=["GET", "POST"])
@login_required
def dashboard():
    if request.method == "POST":
        title = request.form["title"]
        description = request.form["description"]
        new_task = Task(title=title, description=description,
user_id=current_user.id)
        db.session.add(new_task)
        db.session.commit()
        return redirect(url_for("dashboard"))

    tasks = Task.query.filter_by(user_id=current_user.id).all()
    return render_template("dashboard.html", tasks=tasks)
```

This implementation allows users view, create and edit tasks directly in the web interface.

The use of Bootstrap improves user experience, making the application responsive and visually pleasing without the need to write CSS manually.

The interface is now integrated into the backend, ensuring a dynamic and interactive experience.

CHAPTER 20 – IMPROVING APPLICATION PERFORMANCE

The performance of a web application directly impacts the user experience, response time and scalability. A well-optimized Flask application loads quickly, consumes fewer resources, and handles multiple simultaneous accesses better.

This chapter covers essential strategies for improving Flask's performance, including caching, optimizing database queries, efficient use of assets, and asynchronous requests.

Caching to reduce response time

The cache allows you to store query and processing results, avoiding repetitive executions. This reduces database load and improves application loading speed.

THE Flask-Caching makes it easier to implement caching in routes and functions.

Installing and configuring Flask-Caching

Installation can be done with:

bash

```
pip install flask-caching
```

The initial cache configuration in **config.py** define **the type of storage and expiration time**.

python

```
from flask_caching import Cache
```

```python
cache = Cache(config={"CACHE_TYPE": "simple"}) # For local environment
```

```python
def init_cache(app):
    cache.init_app(app)
```

The cache can be used to store data from **database queries**.

python

```python
from .models import Task
```

```python
@cache.cached(timeout=60, key_prefix="task_list")
def get_cached_tasks(user_id):
    return Task.query.filter_by(user_id=user_id).all()
```

This code stores the query result **for 60 seconds**, avoiding repetitive access to the bank.

The application of **decorator @cache.cached** in routes improves performance by storing generated responses.

python

```python
@app.route("/tasks")
@cache.cached(timeout=30)
def list_tasks():
    tasks = get_cached_tasks(current_user.id)
    return jsonify([{"title": t.title, "description": t.description} for t in tasks])
```

This reduces **unnecessary bank inquiries**, improving API response time.

Optimizing database queries

Poorly structured queries can overload the database, reducing the scalability of the application.

Indexing frequently queried columns

Indexing allows for faster searches in large tables. In the model Task, creating indexes improves query performance.

python

```python
from sqlalchemy import Index


class Task(db.Model):
    id = db.Column(db.Integer, primary_key=True)
    title = db.Column(db.String(100), nullable=False)
    completed = db.Column(db.Boolean, default=False)
    user_id = db.Column(db.Integer, db.ForeignKey("user.id"),
nullable=False)


Index("idx_task_user", Task.user_id)
```

This index speeds up searches for tasks for a specific user.

Using lazy loading for relationships

When retrieving a task, Flask-SQLAlchemy can automatically load related user information.

python

```python
class Task(db.Model):
    user = db.relationship("User", backref="tasks", lazy="joined")
```

The use of lazy="joined" avoids multiple queries when loading tasks together with your users.

Results pagination

Applications with large volumes of data should avoid excessive returns. Pagination improves performance by limiting the number of records per request.

python

```python
@app.route("/tasks")
def list_paginated_tasks():
    page = request.args.get("page", 1, type=int)
    per_page = 10
    tasks = Task.query.filter_by(user_id=current_user.id).paginate(page, per_page, False)

    return jsonify([{"title": t.title, "description": t.description} for t in tasks.items])
```

Flask-SQLAlchemy only returns **10 records per request**, reducing memory consumption.

Efficient use of assets and loading optimization

You **assets** include files **CSS, JavaScript and images** used in the application interface.

Static file compression

Files **CSS e JavaScript** should be minified to reduce loading time. Flask-Assets enables this optimization.

bash

```
pip install flask-assets
```

The configuration in **config.py** defines the concatenation and minification of files.

python

```
from flask_assets import Environment, Bundle


assets = Environment()
css = Bundle("styles/main.css", output="gen/main.min.css")
js = Bundle("scripts/main.js", output="gen/main.min.js")


def init_assets(app):
    assets.init_app(app)
    assets.register("css", css)
    assets.register("js", js)
    css.build()
    js.build()
```

This generates optimized files, reducing the size and number of requests to the server.

Asynchronous JavaScript loading

JavaScript can be loaded in a **asynchronous** to avoid blocking page rendering.

html

```html
<script src="scripts/main.min.js" async></script>
```

This approach improves the application's initial loading time.

Asynchronous requests for better user experience

Asynchronous requests allow actions such as **creating and deleting tasks** occur without reloading the page.

THE **Fetch API** in JavaScript makes calls to the Flask API without interrupting the interface.

javascript

```javascript
async function addTask(title, description) {
    let response = await fetch("/tasks", {
        method: "POST",
        headers: {"Content-Type": "application/json"},
        body: JSON.stringify({title: title, description: description})
    });

    let data = await response.json();
    if (data.message) {
        alert("Task added successfully!");
    }
}
```

HTML integration allows you to create tasks without reloading the page.

html

```
<button onclick="addTask('New Task', 'Description')">Add
Task</button>
```

This approach improves **fluidity and responsiveness** of the application.

Common errors and solutions

Cache does not update automatically

If changed data does not immediately reflect in the interface, you may need to clear the cache manually.

python

```
cache.delete("task_list")
```

This ensures that new data is queried directly from the database.

Slow database queries

If the searches are taking too long, the inclusion of **additional indexes** and **pagination** can improve performance.

python

```
Index("idx_task_completed", Task.completed)
```

This optimizes searches for pending or completed tasks.

Static files do not load correctly

If the browser does not update the compressed files, adding a **timestamp na URL** forces the update.

html

```
<link rel="stylesheet" href="gen/main.min.css?
v={{ time.time() }}">
```

This prevents old files from being loaded from the browser cache.

Performance optimization improves response time, scalability and user experience. The use of caching, database indexing, compressed assets and asynchronous requests reduces server load and improves overall application performance.

The implementation of these techniques allows the Flask application to serve a greater volume of users, consume fewer resources and offer a responsive interface.

CHAPTER 21 – ERROR LOGS AND MONITORING

Efficiently debugging a Flask application requires constant monitoring and structured logging. A robust system must be capable of detecting failures, recording critical events, and providing detailed information about errors to facilitate their correction.

The implementation of logs and monitoring ensures that problems can be identified quickly, improving application maintenance and allowing proactive actions to avoid failures in production.

This chapter covers configuring logs, using files to record events, remote monitoring with Sentry, and strategies for capturing and analyzing errors in real time.

Configuring logs for debugging

Logs allow you to record application activities, failures and exceptions in a structured way. Flask uses the standard library logging to store information about the operation of the system.

Configuring basic logs in Flask

The first step is to configure a **log file** to record important events.

python

```
import logging
from flask import Flask


app = Flask(__name__)
```

```
logging.basicConfig(
    filename="app.log",
    level=logging.INFO,
    format="%(asctime)s - %(levelname)s - %(message)s"
)


@app.route("/")
def home():
    app.logger.info("Home page accessed")
    return "Welcome to Task Manager!"
```

This setting defines that events will be written to the file app.log, including the date, severity level and associated message.

Applying log levels ensures that only relevant information is recorded. The main levels are:

- **DEBUG** – Details about the internal workings of the code
- **INFO** – Informational events, such as successful accesses
- **WARNING** – Signs of possible problems, but no immediate impact
- **ERROR** – Errors that require attention but do not interrupt execution
- **CRITICAL** – Serious faults that could compromise the system

Setting the level **INFO** no basicConfig() prevents debug logs from being recorded, reducing file size.

Storing logs in different files

In large applications, storing all logs in a single file can make analysis difficult. For better organization, logs can be separated by event type.

python

```python
error_handler = logging.FileHandler("errors.log")
error_handler.setLevel(logging.ERROR)


app.logger.addHandler(error_handler)
```

Now, the **errors will be stored separately in the file** errors.log, while general events will continue in app.log.

Monitoring exceptions and critical failures

Catching exceptions ensures that **unexpected failures are logged**, preventing silent errors from harming the application.

python

```python
@app.errorhandler(Exception)
def handle_exception(e):
    app.logger.error(f"Error detected: {str(e)}")
    return "An internal error occurred", 500
```

This configuration records **any unhandled exception** and returns an HTTP 500 error to the user.

Logs can also capture **specific errors**, such as failures when accessing the database.

python

```python
@app.route("/db_test")
def db_test():
    try:
```

```
    result = db.session.execute("SELECT * FROM tasks")
    return str(result.fetchall())
except Exception as e:
    app.logger.error(f"Database error: {str(e)}")
    return "Error accessing database", 500
```

Like this, allows **identify flaws in SQL queries and take corrective action** quickly.

Remote monitoring with Sentry and other tools

THE **Sentry** is a powerful tool for remote monitoring, allowing you to capture **errors in real time, analyze metrics and receive automatic alerts** on critical problems.

Installing and configuring Sentry

The first step is to install the official library.

bash

```
pip install sentry-sdk
```

The configuration in **app.py** allows you to capture errors automatically.

python

```
import sentry_sdk
from sentry_sdk.integrations.flask import FlaskIntegration

sentry_sdk.init(
    dsn="https://SEU_DSN_SENTRY",
    integrations=[FlaskIntegration()],
```

```
traces_sample_rate=1.0
)
```

THE **DSN** (Data Source Name) is a unique identifier provided by Sentry to connect your application to the monitoring service.

After this configuration, **any critical error will be sent to the Sentry dashboard**, allowing detailed analysis.

Catching custom errors

In addition to automatic errors, Sentry can be used to **log manual events**, such as specific failures in external integrations.

python

```python
@app.route("/external_api")
def external_api():
    try:
        response = requests.get("https://api.invalida.com")
        response.raise_for_status()
    except requests.exceptions.RequestException as e:
        sentry_sdk.capture_exception(e)
        return "Error accessing external API", 500
```

Phermit **monitor problems with external services** and identify failure patterns.

Log viewing and analysis

Log analysis can be done using tools such as **Logrotate, ELK Stack e Prometheus**, allowing you to view events in real time and detect error patterns.

Using Logrotate to manage log files

THE **Logrotate** prevents log files from growing indefinitely, ensuring that old records are automatically archived.

Basic configuration in Linux can be done by creating a file /etc/logrotate.d/flask_app:

two

```
/var/log/flask/app.log {
    weekly
    rotate 4
    compress
    I'm missing
    notifempty
}
```

That **keeps logs for 4 weeks, compressing old versions** and avoiding excessive space consumption.

Common errors and solutions

Log is not being written to file

If the logs do not appear in the defined file, check whether the write permission is correct.

bash

```
sudo chmod 666 app.log
```

This ensures that the application can **write to log file**.

Errors are not being captured correctly

If exception catching is not working, you may need to increase the logging level.

python

```
app.logger.setLevel(logging.DEBUG)
```

This allows you to record **additional details**, making debugging easier.

Logs grow very fast and consume space

If log files grow quickly, auto-rotation can be configured in Flask.

python

```
from logging.handlers import RotatingFileHandler


handler = RotatingFileHandler("app.log", maxBytes=1000000, backupCount=5)
app.logger.addHandler(handler)
```

This configuration **Limits the size of each file and maintains automatic backups**, avoiding excessive space consumption.

The implementation of structured logs and remote monitoring ensures that faults are detected quickly, avoiding negative impacts on the application.

The use of Flask-Caching to optimize logs, Logrotate to manage files, Sentry for remote monitoring and proactive error capture These are essential practices to ensure the stability of the application in production.

CHAPTER 22 – ADVANCED SECURITY FOR FLASK APPLICATIONS

The security of a web application is one of the most critical aspects of development, ensuring that sensitive data is protected, access is controlled and attacks are mitigated. Flask applications need good protection practices against known vulnerabilities, as well as efficient management of permissions and authentication.

This chapter covers essential strategies for securing a Flask application, including measures against common attacks, implementing secure authentication, and managing permissions.

Good practices and protection against common attacks

The most common attacks against web applications include SQL Injection, Cross-Site Scripting (XSS), Cross-Site Request Forgery (CSRF) e ataques de força bruta. Implementing appropriate protections significantly reduces your application's exposure to these threats.

SQL Injection Prevention

THE **SQL Injection** occurs when user input is entered directly into SQL queries without proper validation, allowing malicious commands to be executed.

The use of **ORMs como SQLAlchemy** avoids this type of vulnerability, as all queries are automatically parameterized.

python

```python
def get_user_by_username(username):
    return User.query.filter_by(username=username).first()
```

This approach prevents the insertion of **malicious SQL codes** directly in the consultation.

In direct SQL queries, **always use safe parameters** instead of string concatenation.

python

```python
db.session.execute("SELECT * FROM users WHERE username = :username", {"username": username})
```

This practice prevents an attacker from being able to modify the SQL query.

Cross-Site Scripting (XSS) Protection

THE **XSS** occurs when unsanitized input is displayed directly in HTML pages, allowing an attacker to insert **malicious scripts**.

Flask protects against XSS when rendering templates with **Jinja2**, automatically escaping variable values.

html

```html
<p>Welcome, {{ user.username }}</p>
```

The content of the variable user.username will be treated as plain text, preventing malicious scripts from running.

If you need to allow secure HTML to be displayed, use |safe only at controlled values.

html

```html
<p>{{ user.bio | safe }}</p>
```

User input must always be validated and sanitized before being stored in the database.

Cross-Site Request Forgery (CSRF) Prevention

THE **CSRF** occurs when an authenticated user performs involuntary actions on a system without their consent.

THE **Flask-WTF** provides automatic protection against CSRF in forms.

bash

```
pip install flask-wtf
```

The configuration in config.py activates this protection.

python

```
class Config:
    SECRET_KEY = "supersecretkey"
    WTF_CSRF_ENABLED = True
```

In templates, each form must include a **token CSRF** to validate requests.

html

```
<form method="POST">
    {{ form.hidden_tag() }}
    <input type="text" name="title">
    <button type="submit">Submit</button>
</form>
```

This ensures that only legitimate requests are processed by the application.

Protection against brute force attacks

Brute force attacks try to guess **user passwords** repeating credential combinations.

The implementation of **attempt limits and temporary blocks** prevents this type of attack.

THE **Flask-Limiter** allows you to restrict the number of attempts per user or IP.

bash

```bash
pip install flask-limiter
```

The initial configuration sets a limit of **5 login attempts per minute**.

python

```python
from flask_limiter import Limiter
from flask_limiter.util import get_remote_address


limiter = Limiter(get_remote_address, default_limits=["5 per minute"])


@app.route("/login", methods=["POST"])
@limiter.limit("5 per minute")
def login():
    # Authentication logic
    return "Login endpoint"
```

If a user exceeds the limit, the API returns an error **429 Too Many Requests**, temporarily blocking further attempts.

Permissions management and secure access

Access control defines **who can access certain features of the application**. This ensures that **only authorized users perform critical operations**.

Secure authentication with Flask-Login and bcrypt

THE **Flask-Login** facilitates user session management, while **bcrypt** ensures that passwords are stored securely.

Installing the libraries is done with:

bash

```
pip install flask-login flask-bcrypt
```

The initial Flask-Login configuration defines the user class.

python

```
from flask_login import UserMixin, LoginManager


login_manager = LoginManager()


class User(db.Model, UserMixin):
    id = db.Column(db.Integer, primary_key=True)
    username = db.Column(db.String(50), unique=True, nullable=False)
    password = db.Column(db.String(100), nullable=False)
```

The user password must be stored securely using **bcrypt**.

python

```
from flask_bcrypt import Bcrypt


bcrypt = Bcrypt()


def register_user(username, password):
    hashed_password =
bcrypt.generate_password_hash(password).decode("utf-8")
    user = User(username=username,
password=hashed_password)
    db.session.add(user)
    db.session.commit()
```

Upon login, password verification occurs with check_password_hash.

python

```
def authenticate(username, password):
    user = User.query.filter_by(username=username).first()
    if user and bcrypt.check_password_hash(user.password,
password):
        return user
    return None
```

This prevents passwords from being stored in clear text in the database.

Implementing roles and permissions

The differentiation of **user roles** allows you to restrict certain actions to only **administrators**.

In the user model, adding a field role defines the access level.

python

```python
class User(db.Model, UserMixin):
    id = db.Column(db.Integer, primary_key=True)
    username = db.Column(db.String(50), unique=True, nullable=False)
    password = db.Column(db.String(100), nullable=False)
    role = db.Column(db.String(20), default="user")
```

Permission validation can be done with a **decorator** which checks if the user has access.

python

```python
from functools import wraps
from flask_login import current_user

def admin_required(fn):
    @wraps(fn)
    def wrapper(*args, **kwargs):
        if current_user.role != "admin":
            return "Access Denied", 403
        return fn(*args, **kwargs)
    return wrapper
```

```python
@app.route("/admin/dashboard")
@login_required
@admin_required
def admin_dashboard():
    return "Admin panel"
```

This ensures that **Only administrators can access certain routes**.

Common errors and solutions

CSRF token missing

If a POST request fails with this error, check whether the HTML template contains the hidden_tag().

html

```html
<form method="POST">
    {{ form.hidden_tag() }}
</form>
```

Without this token, Flask rejects the request for security reasons.

Password stored without hash

If passwords are being recorded in the bank without encryption, the problem may be with the user registry.

Verification can be done by printing the password saved in the bank. If it is readable, use **bcrypt** to store it correctly.

python

```python
hashed_password = bcrypt.generate_password_hash(password).decode("utf-8")
```

Erro 429 Too Many Requests

If legitimate users are being blocked by too many failed attempts, increase the limit in Flask-Limiter.

python

```python
limiter.limit("10 per minute")
```

Like this, it prevents legitimate users from being prevented from accessing the application.

Implementing good security practices, attack prevention and permissions management strengthens the application against threats. The use of protections against XSS, CSRF, SQL Injection, secure authentication and limiting login attempts prevents common vulnerabilities, ensuring that the application works securely and reliably.

CHAPTER 23 – SCALABILITY AND CLOUD INTEGRATION

The scalability of a Flask application is essential to ensure that it can handle a large number of simultaneous requests without degrading performance. As traffic increases, computing resources must be allocated efficiently, ensuring high availability and stability.

This chapter explores strategies for scaling Flask applications, including load balancing, running multiple instances, using scalable databases, and integrating with cloud services like AWS and Google Cloud.

How to scale Flask applications for high traffic

Scalability can be divided into **two main approaches**:

- **Vertical scalability** – Increases the computing power of the server by adding more CPU, RAM and storage.
- **Horizontal scalability** – Adds new application instances and distributes traffic between them.

A **horizontal scalability** is more efficient for Flask applications, as it allows you to distribute the load across multiple servers, reducing the impact of increased users.

Running multiple instances with Gunicorn

Flask has a **embedded server**, but it is not suitable for production. THE **Gunicorn (Green Unicorn)** allows you to run multiple instances of the Flask application on **parallel**, improving performance.

Installation can be done with:

bash

```
pip install gunicorn
```

Running the application with **four workers** improves responsiveness when dealing with multiple requests.

bash

```
gunicorn -w 4 -b 0.0.0.0:8000 app:app
```

Each worker represents a **separate process** running the Flask application, allowing greater parallelism in request processing.

Implementing a load balancer

Or distributed load balancer **requests between multiple application instances**, ensuring that no server is overloaded.

No **NGINX**, the balancing configuration can be defined in the file /etc/nginx/nginx.conf.

nginx

```
upstream flask_app {
    server 127.0.0.1:8001;
    server 127.0.0.1:8002;
    server 127.0.0.1:8003;
}

server {
    listen 80;
    location / {
        proxy_pass http://flask_app;
```

```
    }

}
```

Each Flask instance will run on a different port and the NGINX will automatically distribute traffic between them.

The balancer can be configured to use strategies like round-robin or least connections, ensuring better load distribution.

Use of scalable databases

Database scalability is essential to avoid bottlenecks when the volume of users increases.

THE PostgreSQL and the MySQL support read and write replication, allowing multiple database servers share the query load.

The configuration in **Flask-SQLAlchemy** can be adjusted to use multiple database servers.

python

```
SQLALCHEMY_DATABASE_URI = "mysql://
user:password@master-db/flask_app"
SQLALCHEMY_BINDS = {
    "read": "mysql://user:password@read-replica/flask_app"
}
```

Like this, the application is allowed write to the main bank and read from replicas, better distributing traffic.

Integration with AWS and Google Cloud

Accommodation in climbable clouds allows the application automatically adjust resources according to demand, avoiding infrastructure waste.

Deploy no AWS Elastic Beanstalk

THE AWS Elastic Beanstalk facilitates automatic deployment of Flask applications by managing servers, load balancers, and databases.

Installing the AWS Elastic Beanstalk CLI can be done with:

bash

```
pip install awsebcli
```

The command below **initialize the application in Elastic Beanstalk.**

bash

```
eb init -p python-3.8 flask-app --region us-east-1
```

The deployment is done with:

bash

```
eb create flask-env
```

Oh AWS **will automatically scale** the application as traffic increases, distributing instances across multiple servers.

Using Scalable Databases on AWS

THE **Amazon RDS** allows you to store data in **scalable banks**, automatically configuring read replicas.

The connection string configuration in Flask can be adjusted to use RDS.

python

```
SQLALCHEMY_DATABASE_URI = "postgresql://
user:password@rds-instance.amazonaws.com/flask_app"
```

Deploy no Google Cloud App Engine

THE **Google Cloud App Engine** allows you to host the Flask application without the need to manually configure servers.

The first step is to install the Google Cloud SDK:

bash

```
pip install google-cloud-sdk
```

The file app.yaml defines the environment configuration in Google Cloud.

yaml

```
runtime: python39

entrypoint: gunicorn -b :$PORT app:app

instance_class: F2

automatic_scaling:

  target_cpu_utilization: 0.65

  min_instances: 1

  max_instances: 5
```

The deployment is done with:

bash

```
gcloud app deploy
```

Like this, **automatically provisions servers**, ensuring that the Flask application scales as needed.

Response time optimization

Scalability does not only depend on infrastructure, but also on internal optimizations in the application.

Using distributed cache with Redis

THE **Redis** allows you to store frequently accessed data, reducing the number of database queries.

Installation can be done with:

bash

```
pip install redis flask-caching
```

The configuration in **Flask** uses Redis to store request responses.

python

```
from flask_caching import Cache

cache = Cache(config={"CACHE_TYPE": "redis",
"CACHE_REDIS_URL": "redis://localhost:6379/0"})
cache.init_app(app)

@app.route("/tasks")
@cache.cached(timeout=60)
def list_tasks():
    return get_tasks_from_database()
```

This prevents **Repeated requests overload the database**.

Asynchronous task execution with Celery

THE **Celery** allows time-consuming tasks to be performed **in the background**, preventing the application from being blocked.

Installation can be done with:

bash

```
pip install celery
```

Initial setup connects the **Celery ao Redis**, allowing asynchronous execution of tasks.

python

```python
from celery import Celery

celery = Celery("flask_app", broker="redis://localhost:6379/0")

@celery.task
def process_large_task(data):
    # Heavy processing
    return "Task Completed"
```

The task call occurs without blocking the application.

python

```python
task = process_large_task.delay(data)
```

This improves the user experience by allowing **process long operations without affecting response time**.

Common errors and solutions

Flask application does not scale correctly

If the **load balancer** is not distributing requests, check that the Flask instances have been correctly configured.

bash

```bash
ps to | grep gunicorn
```

If only **an instance is running**, increase the number of workers.

bash

```
gunicorn -w 8 -b 0.0.0.0:8000 app:app
```

This improves the application's responsiveness.

Overloaded database

If bank queries are slow, using **Redis as cache** can lighten the load.

python

```python
@cache.cached(timeout=120, key_prefix="task_list")
def get_tasks():
    return Task.query.all()
```

Prevents the application from accessing the bank unnecessarily.

Scalability ensures that the Flask application can serve thousands of users without loss of performance. Implementing load balancers, scalable databases, caching with Redis, and asynchronous processing with Celery allows you to handle high traffic loads efficiently.

Integration with AWS and Google Cloud provides flexible and scalable infrastructure, ensuring high availability and security for Flask applications in production.

CHAPTER 24 – PUBLISHING AND MAINTAINING THE APPLICATION

Publishing a Flask application involves preparing the production environment, code versioning, final testing and continuous deployment strategies. Keeping an application live requires frequent updates, bug fixes and constant monitoring, ensuring that users always have access to a stable and efficient system.

This chapter covers best practices for versioning, running tests before publication and strategies for continuous deployment, allowing updates to be applied securely and without service interruptions.

Code versioning and maintenance

Code versioning allows you to track changes, roll back changes when necessary, and collaborate in an organized way. THE **Git** is the standard tool for code versioning, allowing full control over development history.

Git configuration and good versioning practices

The first step to keeping your code versioned is to ensure that the repository is configured correctly.

bash

```
git init

git remote add origin https://github.com/seu-repositorio/flask-app.git
```

The repository structure must follow **good practices**, with clear separation between source code, tests and configurations.

arduino

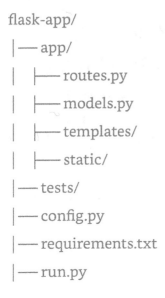

```
flask-app/
|—— app/
|    ├──── routes.py
|    ├──── models.py
|    ├──── templates/
|    ├──── static/
|—— tests/
|—— config.py
|—— requirements.txt
|—— run.py
```

Commits must be organized and contain descriptive messages.

bash

```
git commit -m "User authentication implementation"
```

The creation of **branches** for new features allows you to test changes before final implementation.

bash

```
git checkout -b feature/autenticacao
```

After validating the functionality, the code can be merged into the main branch.

bash

```
git checkout main
git merge feature/authentication
```

This approach prevents untested changes from directly impacting production code.

Final tests before deployment

Testing before publication ensures that the application works correctly and that **no update causes unexpected crashes**.

Running unit tests with Pytest

THE **Pytest** allows you to test individual functions and verify that the results are correct.

Installation can be done with:

bash

```
pip install pytest
```

Tests are organized within the folder tests/, with files named as test_*.py.

python

```
from app import app


def test_home():
    client = app.test_client()
    response = client.get("/")
    assert response.status_code == 200
```

Test execution is done with:

bash

```
pytest
```

If all tests pass, the deployment can be carried out safely.

Integration tests for APIs

Flask APIs can be tested by sending **simulated requests** and checking the answers.

python

```
def test_create_task():
    client = app.test_client()
    response = client.post("/tasks", json={"title": "Nova Tarefa"})
    assert response.status_code == 201
```

This test ensures that task creation works correctly before publishing the application.

Continuous deployment strategies

Continuous deployment automates the publication of new versions of the application, ensuring that updates quickly reach users without interruptions.

CI/CD Setup with GitHub Actions

THE **GitHub Actions** allows you to create pipelines to test and publish the application automatically.

The file .github/workflows/deploy.yml defines the deployment flow.

yaml

```
name: Deploy Flask App

on:
  push:
    branches:
      - main
```

```yaml
jobs:
  deploy:
    runs-on: ubuntu-latest

    steps:
      - name: Code checkout
        uses: actions/checkout@v2

      - name: Configure Python
        uses: actions/setup-python@v2
        with:
          python-version: '3.8'

      - name: Install dependencies
        run: |
          pip install -r requirements.txt

      - name: Run tests
        run: |
          pytest

      - name: Deploy for server
        run: |
```

```
ssh user@servidor "cd /app && git pull && systemctl
restart flask-app"
```

This configuration ensures that whenever there is a push to the main branch, the tests will be automatically executed and the application will be published.

Deploy automatizado no AWS Elastic Beanstalk

THE **AWS Elastic Beanstalk** automatically manages servers, simplifying application publishing.

Installing the AWS Beanstalk CLI can be done with:

bash

```
pip install awsebcli
```

The environment initialization occurs with:

bash

```
eb init -p python-3.8 flask-app --region us-east-1
```

The deployment is done with:

bash

```
eb deploy
```

AWS Elastic Beanstalk will take care of infrastructure provisioning, scaling the application as needed.

Post-deploy monitoring

After publication, it is essential to monitor the application to identify **possible failures and errors** quickly.

Configuring logs in production

Application logs must be stored to **analyze faults and diagnose**

problems.

The logging configuration in config.py can be done with:

python

```
import logging

logging.basicConfig(
    filename="flask-app.log",
    level=logging.INFO,
    format="%(asctime)s - %(levelname)s - %(message)s"
)
```

This ensures that **critical events and errors are automatically logged**.

Monitoring with Prometheus and Grafana

THE **Prometheus** allows you to capture application usage metrics, while **Grafana** displays this information in real time.

Installation can be done with Docker.

bash

```
docker run -d -p 9090:9090 prom/prometheus
docker run -d -p 3000:3000 grafana/grafana
```

The configuration in prometheus.yml defines metrics collection.

yaml

```
scrape_configs:
  - job_name: 'flask'
```

```
static_configs:
  - targets: ['localhost:5000']
```

This allows you to monitor performance metrics and detect bottlenecks in the application.

Common errors and solutions

Deploy failure due to missing dependencies

If the application fails to launch on the server, verify that all dependencies are installed.

bash

```
pip install -r requirements.txt
```

If there are version conflicts, the use of **virtualenv** can help.

bash

```
python -m venv venv
source venv/bin/activate
pip install -r requirements.txt
```

This ensures that **all correct dependencies are loaded into the virtual environment**.

Erro 502 Bad Gateway no NGINX

If NGINX displays error **502 Bad Gateway**, you may need to restart the Flask application.

bash

```
systemctl restart flask-app
```

Checking the Gunicorn status can identify faults.

bash

```
ps to | grep gunicorn
```

If no process is running, Gunicorn must be started manually.

bash

```
gunicorn -w 4 -b 0.0.0.0:8000 app:app
```

This way, it is guaranteed that **the Flask application is running correctly**.

Publishing and maintaining a Flask application involves code versioning, test execution, automated deployment and continuous monitoring. Implementing CI/CD pipelines ensures that updates are applied securely and without service interruptions.

Post-deploy monitoring allows you to quickly detect failures, ensuring that your Flask application operates reliably and scalably.

CHAPTER 25 – THE FUTURE OF FLASK AND FINAL CONSIDERATIONS

Flask has evolved significantly over the years, becoming one of the most used frameworks for web development with Python. Its flexibility, lightness and adaptability have allowed it to be widely adopted in applications of different scales, from simple projects to large complex systems.

With the advancement of web technologies and modern architectures, Flask continues to reinvent itself, incorporating updated practices and integrating with new approaches, such as Asynchronous APIs, microservices, serverless computing and artificial intelligence.

This chapter presents Flask's future directions, expected challenges in web development, and the best ways to stay up to date in the Python ecosystem.

What to expect from the next versions of Flask?

Flask continues its evolution to offer higher performance, scalable application support and compatibility with modern development standards. Some trends shaping the future of the framework include:

Deeper integration with asynchronous programming

Asynchronous support in Flask has already started to gain ground with the use of async and await in some parts of the framework. Future versions should support **native and more efficient for asynchronous processing**, allowing Flask applications to better handle multiple concurrent requests without relying on external solutions.

Compatibility with **ASGI (Asynchronous Server Gateway Interface)** and servers like **Uvicorn** will allow Flask to perform asynchronous tasks more optimally.

python

```python
from flask import Flask


app = Flask(__name__)


@app.route("/async")
async def async_endpoint():
    return "Flask with async support!"
```

The use of Flask with WebSockets and direct integration with asynchronous tasks will allow you to create more efficient real-time applications.

Improved support for modern architectures

Flask is already widely used in microsserviços, but its support for containers, serverless and edge computing will be enhanced to meet the needs of distributed architectures.

Easy integration with Docker and Kubernetes will make deployment more efficient, ensuring that Flask can be dynamically scaled as application demand grows.

The incorporation of observability and distributed tracing tools will help monitor Flask applications in distributed environments, improving code debugging and optimization.

Security enhancements

With the growing need for data protection, Flask will continue to evolve to offer more robust mechanisms against common attacks, like SQL injection, CSRF and XSS.

The standardization of authentication and authorization via OAuth2 and JWT will be increasingly integrated into the framework, allowing developers to implement security without complications.

Compatibility with advanced authentication protocols, like WebAuthn e OpenID Connect, will be improved, ensuring that Flask applications can offer passwordless login and device-based authentication.

Ways to advance in web development

Web development is constantly evolving, and Flask remains a versatile option for different scenarios. To continue growing as a Flask developer, it is essential **monitor trends and improve practices**.

Exploration of complementary frameworks

Flask is a **microframework**, which means it can be combined with different libraries to meet specific needs. Some of the most promising directions include:

- **FastAPI** – For creating high-performance asynchronous APIs
- **SQLAlchemy 2.0** – For more efficient handling of databases
- **Celery e Redis** – For asynchronous processing and task queues
- **GraphQL com Flask-GraphQL** – For more flexible and scalable APIs

The combined use of these tools expands **the possibilities of Flask**, allowing it to remain a modern and powerful option for web applications.

Deepening in DevOps and scalability

A deployment automation and monitoring of Flask applications it will be a competitive differentiator for developers who want to create scalable solutions.

Master tools like Docker, Kubernetes, Terraform e CI/CD will allow you to manage Flask applications in distributed environments and integrated with cloud services.

The configuration of automation pipelines for testing and continuous deployment will ensure greater productivity and less risk when delivering code to production.

Exploration of artificial intelligence and machine learning

The integration of artificial intelligence and machine learning models with Flask will continue to be a strong trend. Applications that use real-time data analysis, natural language processing and computer vision can be easily implemented with Flask and libraries like TensorFlow, PyTorch e OpenAI API.

The construction of **Smart and interactive APIs** will allow Flask developers to create innovative solutions, expanding the scope of applications that can be developed with the framework.

Flask has established itself as one of the most efficient options for web development in Python. Its flexibility and compatibility with various technologies ensure that it will continue to be widely adopted in the coming years.

Flask's evolution will keep pace with the advancement of modern web architectures, supporting asynchronous programming, microservices, cloud computing, and artificial intelligence.

To stand out in Flask development, it is essential to adopt good versioning, security and scalability practices, in addition to exploring new integrations that expand the framework's possibilities.

Dominar Flask opens up opportunities to work on innovative projects, developing agile, efficient applications prepared for the future of technology.

FINAL CONCLUSION

Flask has established itself as one of the most versatile and efficient frameworks for web development with Python. Its simplicity, combined with its ability to expand and integrate with other technologies, makes it an ideal choice for both beginner developers and professionals looking to build scalable and performant applications.

Throughout this book, we go through all the essential stages of development with Flask, from installation and configuration to building a complete project, covering fundamental and advanced topics that guarantee complete mastery of the tool.

Next, we will do a **strategic summary** of each chapter, consolidating learning and highlighting the main points that were covered.

Learning summary: from foundation to complete project

Part 1: Flask Fundamentals

The basis of any Flask application is understanding its structure and fundamental concepts.

- **Chapter 1 – Introduction to Flask and Development Environment**
  Flask was introduced as a **powerful microframework**, ideal for lightweight and flexible web applications. We configure the environment with **Virtualenv e Pipenv**, ensuring an organized and sustainable structure. We create our **first Flask application**, running a local server and understanding the initial code organization.

- **Chapter 2 – Basic Structure of a Flask Application**
  We learned about the organization of files, the importance

of **routes and views** and how to use HTTP methods to structure the application. It was explored **rendering HTML pages**, enabling the construction of dynamic interfaces.

- **Chapter 3 – Working with Templates in Flask**
  The use of **Jinja2** was deepened, allowing the **injection of variables into templates**, the reuse of components and the customization of web interfaces.

- **Chapter 4 – Handling Forms and Requests**
  Flask lets you handle **forms and HTTP requests** easily. We saw how to collect user data, work with **GET and POST methods** and validate inputs to prevent errors and vulnerabilities.

- **Chapter 5 – Database in Flask with SQLAlchemy**
  THE **SQLAlchemy** was presented as an essential tool for manipulating databases. We build a database from scratch, apply **CRUD operations (Create, Read, Update, Delete)** and we integrate our applications with persistent storage.

- **Chapter 6 – Flask and REST APIs**
  We create RESTful APIs using Flask, structure endpoints for efficient communication, and explore tools like **Postman e cURL** to test interactions with the API.

Part 2: Building Web Applications

We deepen the practical application of Flask, ensuring security and dynamism in applications.

- **Chapter 7 – Authentication and Access Control**
  Application security was addressed with **login and logout systems**, using **Flask-Bcrypt** for password hashing and **Flask-Login** for session control and authentication.

- **Chapter 8 – Middleware and Security in Flask Applications**
  We implement **middleware for protection**, mitigating CSRF and XSS attacks. Additionally, we apply good security practices in web development with Flask.

- **Chapter 9 – Uploading and Manipulating Files in Flask**

We explore **file upload**, image manipulation and secure storage, ensuring that malicious files do not compromise the application.

- **Chapter 10 – Flask with WebSockets and Real-Time Applications**
  We create applications that use **WebSockets** for real-time communication, developing a **interactive chat** with Flask-SocketIO and integrating dynamic frontend.

Part 3: Advanced Applications with Flask

We expanded Flask's possibilities, preparing applications for a professional environment.

- **Chapter 11 – Automated Tests in Flask**
  We implement **unit and integration tests** with Pytest, ensuring that our applications worked correctly before publication.
- **Chapter 12 – Flask Application Deployment**
  We configure the environment for **deploy to servers like Heroku and Render**, we explored the use of **Docker** for isolation and learned how to deploy applications on VPS servers.
- **Chapter 13 – Flask and Integration with Other Technologies**
  We integrate Flask with **Redis (for caching), Celery (for asynchronous tasks) and MongoDB (NoSQL database)**, increasing the efficiency and scalability of applications.
- **Chapter 14 – Implementing OAuth and JWT Authentication**
  We created a system of **OAuth authentication with Google, Facebook and GitHub**, in addition to implementing **tokens JWT** for secure authorization of users.
- **Chapter 15 – Flask Application with Artificial Intelligence**
  We explore creating a **chatbot com Flask e OpenAI API**, in

addition to the application of **machine learning and image processing with OpenCV**.

Part 4: Building a Complete Project

We consolidate learning by applying everything to create a realistic and scalable project.

- **Chapter 16 – Definition of the Final Project**
  We choose one **challenging project**, we structure the application and organize the functionalities.
- **Chapter 17 – Creating the Application Backend**
  We implement the **database and business logic**, structuring the models correctly.
- **Chapter 18 – Building APIs and Backend Services**
  We create robust RESTful endpoints, ensuring security with authentication and authorization.
- **Chapter 19 – Creating the Web Interface with Flask and Bootstrap**
  We use **Jinja2 e Bootstrap** to develop a dynamic and responsive interface.
- **Chapter 20 – Improving Application Performance**
  We apply techniques of **caching, query optimization and efficient use of assets**.
- **Chapter 21 – Error Logs and Monitoring**
  We configure **logs for debugging and monitoring with Sentry**, allowing failure tracking.
- **Chapter 22 – Advanced Security for Flask Applications**
  We apply **good security practices** to mitigate common vulnerabilities.
- **Chapter 23 – Scalability and Cloud Integration**
  We explore **AWS e Google Cloud**, ensuring that the application could scale as needed.
- **Chapter 24 – Publishing and Maintaining the Application**
  We implement **versioning, final testing and continuous deployment**, ensuring stability and efficiency.
- **Chapter 25 – The Future of Flask and Final**

Considerations

We analyze the **future of Flask**, including new features, asynchronous support, and trends like serverless and microservices.

Reflection on the importance of mastering and applying Flask

Flask is not just a framework, but a powerful ecosystem for creating modern web applications. Mastering its functionalities allows developers to act in different technology sectors, from API development to artificial intelligence and cybersecurity.

The technology market requires professionals who know build agile, secure and scalable applications. Flask stands out for its flexibility, allowing it to be used in projects of any size, from startups to large corporations.

Along this journey, the knowledge acquired allows any developer to have the necessary tools to create innovative and high-performance solutions, standing out in the professional market.

Continuous learning is essential to keep up with the evolution of technology. The knowledge acquired here is just the beginning of a journey full of opportunities.

We thank you for trusting this material to improve your skills and we hope it will be a turning point in your career. Keep exploring, practicing and developing innovative solutions.

Cordially,
Diego Rodrigues & Team!

www.ingramcontent.com/pod-product-compliance
Lightning Source LLC
LaVergne TN
LVHW051227050326
832903LV00028B/2276